Praise

'*Liberate Your Greatness* is the survival guide that every leader needs to read. In fact, leader or not, if you want to fulfil your potential, the strategies and lessons in this book will help you thrive. Having worked with John on multiple occasions, I've experienced his positively infectious enthusiasm and his spirit of excellence. He has gone the extra mile to equip you with the mindset, skillset and toolset that will make you extraordinary – and help you make a positive impact in the world.'
— **Ant Middleton**, soldier, adventurer, leader and *Sunday Times* bestselling author of *First Man In*, *The Fear Bubble*, *Zero Negativity* and *Mental Fitness*

'When it comes to personal mastery and professional excellence, John Roussot is a Key Person of Influence in this space, and his book *Liberate Your Greatness* is the guide that every entrepreneur and commercial leader needs. John's signature Liberating Greatness Framework and coaching programmes have won international awards, in recognition of the positive impact his work is having in the world. If you're ready to unlock your full potential, make a meaningful impact and take people on the journey with you, this is your roadmap. It's a game-changer.'
— **Daniel Priestley**, co-founder, Dent Global, and bestselling author of *Key Person of Influence*

T0323076

'You always get better when you work with people who expect excellence. John expects excellence and will inspire, challenge and encourage you to strive for excellence in all you do. *Liberate Your Greatness* is an outstanding book that will unlock new levels of success and significance in your personal and professional performance. It's a must-read for all leaders wanting to achieve extraordinary things.'
— **Randy Garn**, *New York Times* bestselling author of *Prosper: Create the life you really want*, serial entrepreneur, investor, and business and life strategist

'As leaders, we all want to serve others to the best of our abilities, maximise our leadership potential and make a positive impact along the way. The problem is, the journey to achieve that can be a lonely road to travel, full of uncertainty, blind spots and self-doubt. Thankfully, you can now have John in your corner to show you the way. As someone who has managed to turn the tide himself and has worked with countless business leaders to help them align and galvanise their team towards a common goal to increase productivity and team morale, John has managed to somehow bottle up a road map to unleash the greatness in all of us. From case studies to anecdotes, tips to strategies, John's practical advice and energetic guidance is not just refreshing, it's quite frankly life-changing.'
— **Mark Leruste**, CEO, Storycast®, and bestselling author of *Glow in the Dark*

'John Roussot's *Liberate Your Greatness* masterfully reveals the profound path from insight to implementation and impact. It guides readers to discover greater awareness and alignment to take positive actions that move them from their current situation to their desired future reality. In this era of accelerating change, having the right strategies and guiding principles is essential for personal and professional success. If you're seeking to create opportunities for growth with greater clarity and acceleration, to smash your goals, this book will prove indispensable.'

— **Sophie Milliken MBE**, CEO, Moja, award-winning entrepreneur, and author of *From Learner to Earner* and *The Ambition Accelerator*

'As a former NFL athlete and competitor on three national television shows, I have come to learn a few things about greatness. In my opinion, it's the key to joyful experiences and a life worth telling a story about, and I love this book because it's a look behind the curtain of what it really takes to liberate your own greatness. John has delivered a game-changer in this book, for anyone looking to access and experience the next levels of greatness in all areas of their life.'

— **Anthony Trucks**, speaker, coach and bestselling author of *Identity Shift*

'John Roussot has a true passion for helping others reach their full potential, and it shines through in *Liberate Your Greatness*. I've worked with John one-on-one as a coaching client of his, and he was a huge help to me. This book includes many of the principles he uses in coaching – and his system gets results!'
— **Amelia Forczak**, founder, Pithy Wordsmithery

'John has, for as long as I can remember, wanted to liberate greatness within people, knowing and believing that within each one of us, lies that special potential. Beyond knowledge, *Liberate Your Greatness* will give you a pathway for a new journey, breaking some shackles as it guides you to reach new heights.'
— **Shaun Lewarne**, Head of Operations, Rivers Church

'This book is a liberating read that I strongly believe will enable you to unleash your full personal and professional potential. Anyone who reads *Liberate Your Greatness* will be left reaping the benefits for years to come and will be inspired to take the necessary steps to elevate themself and positively impact those around them.'
— **Arthur Stamatis**, founder and CEO,
    Home Ice Cream SA

Accelerate your growth.
Achieve your goals faster.
Amplify your impact.

LIBERATE YOUR
GREATNESS

JOHN
ROUSSOT

R^ethink

First published in Great Britain in 2023
by Rethink Press (www.rethinkpress.com)

© Copyright John Roussot

Cover photography by Jo Scott Images

*I dedicate this book to my lovely wife, Daleen, and our
precious children, Jewel, Anthony and Marcus.
You are my everything and why I do what I do.*

*To Tony and Tulla Roussot, thank you for being incredible
role models, giving all you had to give, and teaching me to
live, learn, love and grow every day.*

*To all the visionary, humble and engaging leaders seeking
to learn and grow personally and professionally and take
others on the journey with you, I exist to serve you and
liberate your greatness.*

Contents

Foreword

This book is written for you. As the saying goes, 'When the student is ready, the teacher will appear.' If you are seeking a kind of business or personal renewal to reframe your thinking – to challenge yourself to liberate the greatness that you have always suspected is latent within you – then John Roussot's masterly step-by-step guide is for you.

John will not only share his proven methodology, but he will also challenge you each step of the way. What I love about my time with John is that he treats every coaching session as a first, showing up with enthusiasm and excellence. His boundless energy is reflected in the pages that follow with stories, anecdotes and examples of people liberating their greatness by applying his rigour. Page after page, John will be fresh and challenging. Are you ready?

I have been a student for most of my life and getting better each year as I more intensely focus my curiosity on my evolving world and the many fascinating issues and circumstances that life throws my way. My friend and coach, John listens intently to my thoughts on specific topics and gently presses me to dive deeper into them, with often quite revealing 'ah-ha' moments. I have never thought so deeply as I have through the questioning, patience, role modelling and encouragement that John offers.

I have managed and led many great people throughout Asia Pacific for more than ten years, and throughout Europe, the Middle East, Africa and India for more than twenty-five years. To me, life is 'all about the people', and business is no exception. I love to see people grow and realise their best selves. Over the past few years working with John, I have seen more of our tribe grow in stature and confidence – to some, the experience has been life changing.

My purpose is to create an environment where people can thrive; a place where people feel psychologically safe to share their ideas without intimidation or fear but with encouragement and support. I do this through being thoughtful, engaging and Socratic, giving people time and listening to them. This has always been my way, however I have only recently been able to articulate this, and – with John's masterly coaching – purposefully develop my expertise.

Wonderfully, sharing and asking your colleagues and family about the three words that might reflect their essence leads to amazing conversations. Your three words are not hard and fast, although centring on them brings real focus and clarity.

You will see from the contents list that the chapters in this book are well set out with a clear road map to liberating your greatness. This is not a novel, so I recommend that you take your journey of mastering on a week-by-week basis, or a cadence that allows you to assimilate and practise. This has been my journey – one that has been shared by many of my tribemates. Challenge yourself to explore your deepest thinking about each question. This will help you to identify preferences in your personal style and identify the key habits to build upon as you liberate your greatness.

I wish you great learning.

William (Bill) Noble, Group Managing Director, WD-40 Company Ltd

Introduction

Greatness is within you. To enable you to liberate it, all you need are the right strategies, perspectives and challenges. I want to help you to tap into your full potential and live a life of greatness – one where you have more clarity, confidence, courage and connection.

What I'm about to share with you has truly life-changing possibilities. Apply the principles in this book and you will accelerate your growth, achieve your goals faster and amplify your impact.

You will need to reflect on some profound questions:

- Who do you want to become?

- What do you want to achieve?

- What impact do you want to have in the world?

The Liberating Greatness Framework® I'm going to give you in this book contains universal truths that I've learnt from some of the greatest individuals and businesses around the world. It also contains my best insights, models and principles to help you succeed personally and professionally. *Liberate Your Greatness* is for you and every leader. To do more and contribute more, you must first become more.

Whether you're a leader in a large corporate organisation, a business owner, an entrepreneur, a team leader or a leader in your community or family, I value your investment in your personal and professional development. I honour you for your vision, humility and desire to learn and grow.

Your next level depends on your ability to successfully lead, connect, inspire, encourage and uplift others. When they succeed, you'll succeed. You may already be an achiever or have ambitions to get to even higher levels of personal and professional performance to create a better future for yourself, your family, your team or your business.

Having worked with thousands of people in thirty-three countries, I've had the privilege of engaging with outstanding business leaders who've embraced opportunities to help their people grow by creating environments for them to thrive.

Over the past two decades, my experience in the corporate world and entrepreneurial ventures, consulting to and coaching individuals, teams and businesses around the world, has given me a unique perspective to share with you. I've seen and experienced global best practices to replicate, and witnessed examples of what not to do when leading people.

In the corporate world, I've worked for Fortune 500 company, P&G; held senior director roles in global companies Kantar, Arla Foods and Reckitt; and consulted to well-known global household brands including Abbott, BP, Coca-Cola, Danone, Dyson, Henkel, Sony, Tesco and WD-40, as well as various national, regional and multinational businesses in the US, UK, Europe, Middle East, Africa and Asia.

As an entrepreneur, I've successfully launched, run and sold a couple of businesses, and I've also been involved in business ventures that failed. These successes and failures have helped me gain resilience, insight and empathy into the struggles that so many people are facing in tough social and economic environments around the world. I've had many ups and downs, both personally and professionally.

As an executive high-performance coach and trainer, I have the pleasure and privilege of liberating greatness for the incredible entrepreneurs, business leaders and their teams that I'm blessed to work with. As an international speaker and author, I'm grateful for you, dear reader, for the opportunity to serve you by unleashing your greatness.

We are kindred spirits on a quest for continual learning and development. Excellence is the gradual result of always striving to be better; having the humility to test, learn and grow through experiences as we acquire new skills and knowledge and then share them with others to accelerate their own learning curves. There's a significant return on investment (ROI) to be had when investing your time, energy, resources, money and headspace in developing yourself and others. There's also a cost of inaction (COI) when you don't.

Renowned leadership author, speaker and mentor John Maxwell says, 'A leader is one who knows the way, goes the way, and shows the way.'[1] That's the experience you'll have with this book. You will know the way and go the way – learning the strategies, principles, frameworks and practical tools that will liberate greatness in your own life – so that you can become a role model for others and show them the way to their next level too.

So, how can you liberate your greatness and unlock your full potential? How can you positively influence others to embrace your vision, come alongside you and support your dreams? How can you facilitate better clarity, communication and collaboration with your teams, inspire more confidence and courageous action, and ultimately lead yourself and others to new levels of success and significance? We'll answer those questions together as we explore various principles and frameworks.

Reflection is a skill. As you read through the content in this book, reflect on how you might apply the principles to your own life and then put them into practice. Take time to reflect, practise, think and then act – that's how you master any skill. Over time, the principles will become instinctive, and you will naturally apply them consciously and subconsciously.

Strive for personal mastery and professional excellence

There are two main themes that run through this book: personal mastery and professional excellence. When you succeed in your personal life by mastering your health, wealth and relationships, your personal progress positively impacts your professional life. As you strive for excellence in your professional life, the daily, weekly and monthly disciplines and routines you put in place will allow you to amplify your performance and enhance your results at work and in your personal life. There's a beautiful interplay between personal mastery and professional excellence, and I'll share strategies throughout the book on how to thrive in both areas.

Minor tweaks lead to major impact. Applied consistently, the principles and frameworks in this book will help you achieve quick wins that will compound over time. Your interactions and relationships at home and at work will improve. You will be able to engage your people at work better, energise your business, create a culture of high performance and co-create the future.

It all starts with you. This is your moment to step up, serve and lead at higher levels of excellence, and I'm here to coach, challenge, push and support you all the way. Every professional sportsperson has a coach – in fact, they probably have a team of coaches to help them become 1% better every day. Athletes crave feedback,

perspective, best practices and positive challenges because they help fast-track their learning, growth and performance. I want to encourage you to have the same hunger to study and practise the principles I'll share with you throughout this book.

I've distilled all these lessons into a simple framework that is easy for you and your people to master. Simplicity is key to effective execution. I want you to know the principles and apply them, so that you get real results.

The structure of this book

Part One sets the scene for your personal and professional growth, providing the origin story to some of my messaging themes, and the principles, tools and lessons that you'll be able to apply to enable you to excel in your personal and professional lives.

Part Two is all about the information and insights you gain through principles one and two: the Principle of Awareness and the Principle of Alignment. Without mastering these two principles you cannot achieve optimal results, regardless of how hard you work.

Part Three is about implementation and covers principles three and four: the Principle of Action and the Principle of Accountability. The world's highest performers are remarkably focused on the actions they take consistently over the long term, and they value the necessity of accountability to ensure they perform at their best.

Part Four details how to amplify your impact and achieve your goals faster through the Principle of Amplification and the Principle of Acceleration. With the first four principles firmly in place, principles five and six create the long-lasting and powerful ripple effect that you strongly desire.

Each of the principles is powerful on its own and will help you achieve your goals faster, but collectively they will truly liberate your greatness. As John F Kennedy once said, 'A rising tide lifts all boats.'[2] Expect to see enhanced performance in all areas of your life.

Throughout the following chapters, you'll find frameworks and action items to help you achieve quick wins and gain initial momentum. Be intentional about searching for the hidden themes and key insights you'll discover that will unlock new levels of possibility, knowledge, emotion and behaviour. Trust me, trust the process and trust the science… objects in motion tend to stay in motion! When you build momentum, you will achieve phenomenal results. It's time to go to your next level of success and significance, personally and professionally, by unleashing the greatness that is within you.

PART ONE

GREAT EXPECTATIONS

Here's the plan. In Chapter 1, we'll address any fears that may be holding you back. I'll share strategies to help you face them head-on, reminding you that stepping into your potential doesn't have to be scary.

In Chapter 2, I'll guide you on how to strike that elusive balance between your personal and professional lives. Success at home can fuel your achievements at work, and vice versa. I'll show you how intertwining these two key areas can propel you forward, creating a well-rounded journey towards your own greatness.

I have great expectations that you will not only move from good to great, but that you will also discover the extraordinary in you.

ONE

Be Not Afraid Of Greatness

It's your time and everyone's counting on you

Welcome to the starting line. Before we get going, I want to let you in on my personal journey and some of the experiences that have shaped me and driven me to believe that greatness is in all of us, and it can be unlocked.

My experience has also taught me that it is not always lucky breaks that lead to greatness. Sometimes life's catastrophes can be the waymarkers on our journey to a better tomorrow.

I'm not an elite sportsman, a billionaire businessman or a famous singer. As much as I love sport, business and singing, I haven't committed myself to the level required to achieve worldly standards of greatness in those areas... yet. However, I do have a black belt in three styles of karate, I've built a few successful businesses and I've sung at events in beautiful locations around the world. I have achieved many things that speak to my vision of greatness, which have taught, shaped and inspired me to be and do more. As you may be, I'm on a journey to liberating my own greatness, and I'm grateful that we can learn and grow together.

I am blessed in so many ways: I am healthy, happily married with three beautiful children and full of faith, hope and love. Every day of my life, I'm striving to be the GOAT (greatest of all time) that I'm called to be: the greatest husband to Daleen; the greatest father to my kids; the greatest servant leader to my team; the greatest coach, trainer and trusted adviser to my clients and to the people I serve.

How do you define 'greatness'? What internal greatness do you want to unleash in your own life?

Your greatness is yours to discover. As Leo Buscaglia said, 'You are the most beautiful, unique you that has been, and ever will be.'[3] You'll always be the second-best version of anyone else, and everyone else will always be the second-best version of you. When you liberate your greatness, you unlock all of who you are, and give the best of who you are to everyone around you. I want to help you discover the innate greatness you have inside you to give to the world as you become all you're called to be.

Gratitude for humble beginnings

In the late 1960s, my maternal grandparents, Louis and Hariklia Loizides, left their homeland of Cyprus and sailed to the small town of Richards Bay on the north-east coast of South Africa. The town lies next to the deepest natural harbour on the African continent, on a lagoon of the Mhlathuze River. This, combined with its proximity to coal and aluminium mines, attracted wider industry, while inland, sugar farmers created lush green rolling hills of cane and a growing tourism industry billed the town as a 'gateway to Zululand', an area of large game parks and diverse wildlife.

My grandmother used to tell us wonderful stories about how her family and friends in Cyprus thought they were crazy and told them they would be eaten by lions, killed by crocodiles or at least bitten by some kind of deadly snake. Coincidently, lions, crocodiles and deadly snakes were indeed natural inhabitants of Zululand, but my grandparents certainly weren't afraid, and they survived.

Together, they opened the first convenience store in Richards Bay, which sold everything from paraffin (10 cents for 5l) to a whole lamb for ZAR 1 (one South African rand, equivalent to US$0.06 or £0.05 in today's conversion) – according to my grandmother, of course. Over the years, they expanded their service to the community by building a shopping centre, which included a Spar, the town's first supermarket.

Their daughter Tulla married my father Tony, and they too moved to Richards Bay, where my father joined the family business and worked in the Spar with my mother's brothers, Alex and Chris. Dad had the courage to abandon his engineering studies to follow a more entrepreneurial path. He started working at the back door of the Spar, receiving goods, and slowly worked his way up through the business, eventually buying it from my grandfather and uncles. Together, my parents served the community with purpose, passion, philanthropy and excellence. They were unbelievable role models for me and my siblings, as they demonstrated a strong work ethic, sincere care and an excellent service for their customers.

The Zululand community was close. Growing up there, I learnt the value and true meaning of *ubuntu* – essential human virtues of compassion, humanity and connection. Being a small town, everyone knew everyone in Richards Bay. People had real connections, one-to-one relationships, and families grew up together. Communities gathered in church, the Round Table, the Rotary Club, the Business Women's Association and the Chamber of Commerce, so everyone got to know and support each other well.

A product of my entrepreneurial parents – and possibly as a result of expectations from the community – I became passionate about showing up as the best I could be at a young age. Both at school and on the sports fields, I was always striving to achieve strong results. As a child, I constantly had 100 things on the go, and every weekday involved some form of extracurricular activity. I excelled at rugby, cricket and swimming, and over weekends I water-skied, cycled and went to the gym.

Role models inspire us to be better

Hard work and achievement were especially important to my dad. He was a phenomenal role model, who taught me and pushed me to work harder than the average person so that I would develop my skills and achieve more. He wanted me to be ahead of the curve and knew that talent alone wouldn't be enough.

He loved encouraging me with catchphrases, like 'Work smarter, not harder', and often quoted the great South African golfer, Gary Player, who said, 'The harder I work, the luckier I get.'[4]

My dad was incredibly busy as a business owner, but he always made time for his family. He attended all my sporting events and made my learning and development a priority. He would be on the sidelines, encouraging me, cheering me on and never ridiculing any mistakes, while pushing me to be better with love, encouragement and support.

I can't remember him ever missing me compete. In fact, when I was boarding at senior school, my matches were one and a half to two hours' drive (at best) from Richards Bay. I remember once running onto the rugby field, so angry that he hadn't yet arrived to give me his routine inspiring pep talk before the game. How arrogant and naive I was! I wasn't thinking at all about his work commitments, the traffic en route or the sacrifices he was making to be there for me; I was only thinking about myself. He arrived just after the whistle blew to start the match, and I was unnecessarily grumpy for at least fifteen minutes until I realised he was there, supporting and cheering me on as always, helping me get my head in the game and give my best on and off the field. I didn't appreciate his efforts enough until later in my life.

Mastering the fundamentals

At the age of five I started karate to 'defend my mother from strangers'! (Not that she needed defending from anyone, but I guess it was good motivation to start my journey to receiving a black belt.) It was most likely also Mr Miyagi and Daniel-san from the original *Karate Kid* movie that inspired me to become a karate kid myself. When I started karate, there were around ten of us in my group of friends in the first lesson, which whittled down to around five after the first year, before eventually everyone slowly dropped out. Except for me.

Because I stuck with the lessons twice a week for the next seven years, I mastered the fundamentals of each level, graded through the belts and ultimately became a junior black belt sensei at the age of twelve. This was one of my first life lessons in mastery, where I began to understand the power of habits and small daily actions that compound over time with significant impact – the power of 'Wax on, wax off', as Mr Miyagi would teach.

Throwing combinations of punch-punch, punch-punch, punch-punch for hours on end as a white belt seemed incredibly mundane at the time, which is why all my friends dropped out. They grew bored of the basics. Stack years of mastering the fundamentals and suddenly I got to black belt, where I could throw six punches a second, and then – trust me – things got *way* more exciting! Looking back to the moment I received my black belt, I now realise that was the start of a never-ending journey of discipline, consistent effort and the pursuit of excellence (self-mastery).

We often get tired of the fundamentals, not only in our hobbies but also in our work and daily lives. But there's value in knowing and practising the basics. They're what we come back to instinctively when the pressure is on and we need to perform. If you're not making the progress that you want to – if you're not achieving what you want to achieve – returning to world-class basics almost always gets the results you desire.

Throughout my life, I also cultivated my enjoyment of singing and acting, playing the lead roles of Danny Zuko in *Grease* and Pippin in *Pippin* at senior school. After university I also performed in the Broadway *Parade* musical in Cape Town. I have also sung at private and public events across South Africa and in the UK, including a big band show I created, called *Into the Swing of Things*. Despite having a busy schedule, I managed to find a way to succeed at some level in various areas of my life. I thrived on being busy, productive and effective.

Working through life's unexpected hardships

I began my first corporate job at Procter & Gamble in Cape Town, moved to Johannesburg, and four years into my career, I left to start an entrepreneurial business. Three months into my new project, I remember being at work when I received a phone call that nobody ever wants to receive. It was my uncle Alex, who said to me, 'Johnny, we've lost your dad.'

'Lost him?' I said, my heart pounding in my chest. Thinking maybe he was missing, I asked, 'What do you mean, we've lost him?' Then it hit me. 'Is he dead?'

'Yes,' replied my uncle.

'Was it a heart attack?' I asked.

'No, Johnny. He took his life.'

Those words will echo in my memory forever. I lost my dad to suicide. My role model, my father, my friend, my biggest fan, gone in an instant. I spoke to my mother, who was understandably hysterical. Then

I had to make the toughest two calls of my life: to my siblings to tell them what had happened.

A month before he died, Dad had undergone a back operation that left him feeling physically and mentally incapacitated. As a result – and combined with the cocktail of medication he was on – he felt like he couldn't serve at the levels he wanted to anymore and thought that he was becoming a burden to his family. He was a man of faith and love, but he had lost hope. He had given so much to everyone around him his entire life. The only thing he ever took was his own life.

If only he knew how loved and appreciated he was by his family, his friends and the community. Over 2,000 people attended his funeral, and I know that every one of them would have helped him with whatever he needed, had he just asked.

That dreadful day, I moved back to Richards Bay to pick up the pieces, support my mother and take care of the family coffee shop business. My plan at the time was to steady the ship, sell the coffee shop quickly, move my mother to Johannesburg with me and carry on with the dream life I'd established for myself. However, six months after my dad passed away, my mother was diagnosed with colon cancer. She fought bravely for the next two years before she too passed away.

If you would have told me on the morning of 3 November 2004, while I was working out at the gym or as I was working at the office before I received the call, that within two and a half years I would lose both my parents, would have to give up my perfect life, move back to the small town I had worked so hard to leave and take over a business I didn't want in an industry I knew nothing about, I would have thought you were crazy. But that's exactly what happened.

More than just a coffee shop

I bought the Elephant & I (E&I) coffee shop from my mother before she passed away, realising that there was so much I couldn't control and that I had to work with what was in my hands. Banks wouldn't support me, so I remortgaged my house to raise the funds to buy and renovate the coffee shop. The shopping centre we were in was expanding, with several new national coffee shops and restaurant franchises coming to town, so I knew I needed to upgrade the store if we were going to survive.

I engaged with an architect, Pedro, who had been a family friend for many years, and together we redesigned the entire shop. We ripped up the carpets, tore down the ceilings and bashed through walls to expand our seating capacity from 80 to 120. We changed the layout in the kitchen to include new equipment, a scullery, a freezer and cold storerooms, a dry storeroom and an office, and streamlined our processes to make us more effective and efficient.

The front of house was completely redesigned with curved, welcoming ceiling lines, brand-new good-quality dark wooden chairs and tables, and comfy bench seating around the perimeter of the store, with four cosy corners that were always favourite seating areas for families and team meetings alike. We moved the barista coffee station from the back of the shop to the entrance to create more ambience and in-store theatre.

As you entered the store, you could hear coffee being ground, see the espresso machine pouring and smell freshly baked muffins, scones and cakes, which we made on site every day. Wherever you looked, something appealed to your senses. From the deli and retail section to the pendant lighting; from the unisex restrooms with a large round mosaic basin and handtowels embroidered with our logo to our famous elephant photos, now beautifully framed with spotlights shining on them to give them an exclusive gallery feel. Everything was designed with a clear purpose and this attention to detail set us apart in the industry.

We trained our staff every week to find ways to continually improve our products and services. Our food was outstanding, and our service was excellent because we worked hard at it. We knew that if we operated at the highest levels of excellence and our competition operated at mediocre levels, the gap would be free publicity for us. It was. People soon started speaking about the significantly better experience at the E&I versus our competitors.

I strived to create an excellent experience for customers and staff, and within six months we had doubled monthly sales revenue and tripled the profitability of the business. All while the national chains that opened on our doorstep struggled to make ends meet, and many of them ended up closing their doors.

All things happen for a reason. My coffee shop experience taught me so much about business, customer service and experience, building high-performing teams, and delivering outstanding products and services to beat the competition.

I learnt that when you do things with a spirit of excellence, success gravitates towards you. I also learnt the power of partnering with great people to co-create something special. I have wonderful memories of my time with Pedro, the architect; Graeme, the builder; and Arthur, one of my best friends. (Arthur was a great business mentor to me and even helped me with cashflow to buy stock as we were about to reopen the store after two months of being closed for renovations.) I wouldn't have been able to achieve that level of success without them, my incredible staff who worked so hard to keep my parents' legacy alive, my brother and sister for their moral support, and the support and encouragement of Daleen, my girlfriend at the time, whom I married a year after opening the new store.

As Shakespeare wrote, 'Some are born great, some achieve greatness, and some have greatness thrust upon them. Be not afraid of greatness.'[5] Success to me, despite adversity, is all about interactions with people, the journey to greatness and the lessons learnt along the way.

Courage is acting in spite of fear

The E&I endeavour was a practice in courage. I had to step way out of my comfort zone, and it paid off – not just financially.

I remember a busy Saturday morning at the coffee shop, a year before the renovation. The restaurant was full and people were buzzing, connecting with friends and family. You could hear the coffee grinder and espresso machine working overtime. The smell of freshly baked muffins filtered through the store. Some waitresses were serving breakfasts and coffees, others were taking orders. The kitchen staff were delivering outstanding-quality food at pace, as always. Every-thing was running perfectly by design.

As I was rushing into the kitchen to fetch an order for a customer, out of the corner of my eye, I noticed a beautiful girl looking at me. Our eyes met, I smiled, and a few minutes later I approached her table and asked if she was enjoying her meal. She smiled and said 'Yes.' I left her and her mother, whom she was with, to finish their meals. When I looked across to see her again, she was gone.

Later that day, I was talking to a customer at the front of the store and noticed the same girl walking towards me. She came up to me and said, 'Here, this is for you', and she gave me a CD called *Spirit* by the singer-songwriter, Jewel.

I said, 'Oh, thanks', and she turned around and walked away. I went into my office and opened the CD case. On the inside of the album booklet, followed by her name and telephone number, she'd written, 'Maybe we should go for a coffee sometime?'

Talk about courage. That was a *Sliding Doors* moment, a moment in time that shaped our destinies. How differ-ent our lives would have been had she not demonstrated courage that day!

We went for coffee together and two years later I married my soulmate, Daleen. We settled down and had three children within three and half years, and as my family grew so did my ambition (partly by neces-sity, to provide at a higher level).

After our third child was born, I battled to find the work-life balance I wanted and needed in my corporate job, after having sold the coffee shop to my business part-ner. I quickly found myself overweight, not exercising and in a bad place emotionally, mentally and physically.

I had a strong realisation that something needed to change. When I looked around me, long hours and total exhaustion seemed to be markers of success, with people sacrificing their well-being and relationships in favour of professional progress. Late-night emails were rampant, and projects completed in the early hours of the morning were celebrated in group huddles.

That's when I realised it wasn't just me that needed to change but also the corporate culture and mindset towards performance.

Getting FiiT4GROWTH

I moved to the UK with my family in September 2015 and worked for three different corporate organisations between then and the end of August 2020. Throughout my time in the corporate world, I saw people mentally, emotionally and physically stressed, anxious, depressed, burnt out and fatigued.

I travelled extensively in my global corporate roles, and I found the same to be true in various markets around the world. Corporate cultures were rewarding achievement at all costs. That often resulted in unhealthy attitudes and behaviours and physical and mental health challenges for their people, which in turn negatively impacted their confidence, courage and creativity. Relationships at work and home were being damaged.

Committed to finding solutions, I began to research and study science-backed high-performance coaching curriculums. Busy professionals want and need strategies and tools that are proven to help them achieve heightened and sustained levels of performance.

My quest to find the best performance curriculum on the planet led me to becoming a certified high-performance coach through Brendon Burchard and the High-Performance Institute.

In early 2020, I could feel the burden of what the world was about to experience... a physical health pandemic, a financial pandemic and a mental health pandemic. In my heart and mind, I knew I needed to play whatever role I could to help, because of the pain I experienced with my parents' passing.

Part of my fight now is to help people with their mental, emotional, physical and spiritual well-being. When we entered lockdown for the first time in 2020, I felt called to step out of corporate and serve at a higher level.

At the time, I was working as the global commercial capability director for a multinational consumer goods company. Companies across the UK – and indeed the world – abruptly shut their offices and instructed employees to work from home indefinitely. Stripped of their normal working environments, it was the end of the corporate world as we once knew it.

Employees were left hunched over laptops on kitchen tabletops, glued to screens and anxiety-inducing daily news bulletins, with video calls being their only lifeline to the outside world. Already-exhausted parents juggled virtual school and work deadlines simultaneously and the boundary between our work and our personal lives, which was once blurred, became indistinguishable.

I knew more than ever before that everything I had learnt from training as a high-performance coach, and decades of intentional study and practice of the strategies that lead to success, was critical for survival in this 'new world'.

As the international crisis unfolded before our eyes, I realised how thirsty we were for non-working time and for the experiences we tried to squeeze around the consuming vortex of work. It might have seemed crazy to a lot of people who were holding on to the safety and security of a job, but that was exactly the time I felt I needed to do something different to recalibrate and reprioritise the things that mattered most.

I quit my corporate job and, together with four amazing friends and fellow coaches, launched a free six-week programme of high performance for those in need. We had people registered from the West Coast of the US all the way through to the East Coast of Australia. Some were being made redundant or were on furlough, others were struggling to keep afloat in companies that were affected by the pandemic. Everyone was in the same boat, despite their background, location or vocation. We all needed support, encouragement, strategies and tools to navigate through the storm. That's what we did.

On 1 September 2020, during the global pandemic, with no savings or financial support but equipped with knowledge, purpose, passion, a strong desire to serve (and, of course, my wife's approval), I stepped into my business, FiiT4GROWTH, full-time. I left a global role in a large multinational because I could see people struggling and I had to answer the call to help those in adversity. I wanted to connect, inspire, encourage and uplift. I wanted to provide hope for a better future; share strategies, tools and tangible tactics to help people navigate through unprecedented times so that they could go from survival to success to significance.

I turned pain into purpose and built FiiT4GROWTH around four pillars: personal mastery, professional excellence, commercial excellence and social impact. I'm on a mission to make a positive impact in the world, promoting three of the Global Goals:[6]

- 1 – No poverty

- 3 – Good health and well-being

- 8 – Decent work and economic growth

The power of habit

We saw the benefits that routine, habits, purpose, clarity on who you are and consistently taking small incremental steps towards goals can have on an individual, despite the planet being at a total standstill. It was almost as if the world needed to slow down – no, actually, stop – for people to realise that the small actions they take each day lead to the people they will ultimately become. Daily disciplines compound to create success over time. 'Punch-punch' for years leads to making six punches a second when you've consistently mastered the skill.

It was there that FiiT4GROWTH was truly born. As the pandemic ensued and reversing the equation became the norm, companies realised they needed to embrace individual needs and progress first or watch their performance aspirations go up in flames.

Summary

I have a vision for a world where individuals, teams and businesses can liberate their greatness using the strategies and tools I've had the privilege of implementing in my own life, so that they can achieve their personal and professional goals faster, while maintaining their well-being and relationships.

Everything in my past – the great experiences, adversities, wins and lessons learnt – has created my purpose and passion for people, my fight against mental and physical health issues, and my desire to connect, inspire, encourage and uplift the people around me.

Proverbs 13:22 says, 'A good man leaves an inheritance to his children's children.'[7] Your greatness is a gift for you to give to the world. It should outlive you. You can make a positive impact in the lives of those around you, so that, long after you're gone, people remember that someone, somewhere, sometime made a positive impact that they're now benefiting from. That's what I want for my own life and that's what I want for you too – to live, learn, love and grow every day, so that you leave a legacy of inspiring others to do the same.

It's your time and everyone's counting on you. *Carpe diem*, seize the day. Seize the moment and be the inspiration your family, friends, team, business and community need you to be. Be bold, be brave, be brilliant. Be not afraid of greatness.

TWO

Personal Mastery And Professional Excellence

Your growth is your business

In the pursuit of greatness, the journey towards personal mastery and professional excellence is a critical component of success. In this chapter, we will explore the importance of taking ownership of your personal and professional growth. I want to equip you with some guiding principles to consider as you read this book. By embracing the mindset that your growth is your business, you are not only acknowledging the value of continuous learning and development but also empowering yourself to become the best version of who you are meant to be.

Your growth is your business

As business leaders and entrepreneurs, the responsibility for our own growth and development ultimately falls upon us. It is our obligation to invest in ourselves, expand our skillsets and enhance our knowledge, ensuring that we remain competitive in today's ever-changing world. Strive to achieve personal mastery and professional excellence and you will achieve greatness. That requires a greater mindset, skillset and toolset.

A greater mindset

Your mindset either holds you back or unleashes your full potential, playing a crucial role in determining the trajectory of your life.

A limiting mindset is characterised by thoughts that reinforce self-imposed boundaries and perpetuate the idea that opportunities are scarce. This mindset can create a vicious cycle, where fear of failure and self-sabotage prevent you from realising your dreams and aspirations. If you cultivate a limiting mindset, you may find yourself trapped in self-doubt, fear and negative beliefs that hinder your growth and success.

On the other hand, an empowering mindset embraces possibilities, growth and continuous learning. By adopting this mindset, you develop the confidence to face challenges head-on, learn from your mistakes and consistently strive for self-improvement. An empowering mindset fosters a sense of purpose, determination and adaptability, which enables you to break free from constraints and achieve remarkable accomplishments. By consciously cultivating an empowering mindset, you can overcome obstacles to unlock your true potential, fuelling your motivation, resilience and willingness to take risks in the pursuit of your goals and chart a path towards personal and professional success.

In his book, *Awaken the Giant Within*, Tony Robbins suggests, 'Whatever you focus on you will feel more intensely.'[8] He goes on to explain how your focus and feelings then impact your actions. It all starts with mindset.

Let's do a quick exercise. If you were to look around the room you're in right now, specifically looking at everything you can see that's brown in colour, what do you see?

Now, without looking around the room again, without lifting your eyes from this page, did you notice anything blue? How about green?

Now look around your room and see if you can see anything blue or green. I imagine you found at least a few items you hadn't seen previously.

Often, we choose to focus on all the brown stuff in our lives: the challenges, the obstacles, the hardships. Guaranteed, the media is telling you to focus in on the brown stuff in the world: wars, politics, crime, corruption, death and destruction. I don't want to undermine all the suffering in the world, and my heart goes out to those impacted by wars, diseases, poverty and bad politics, but what about all the good that's happening? What about the everyday heroes that are making a positive impact in their families' lives, in their communities and businesses? What about the bright, bold colours in your own life – the blues and greens? The people that brighten up your day? The moments of joy, gratitude, love, excitement, adventure or celebration?

Like me, I'm sure you have a ton of brown stuff to focus on in your life. It's a choice, though. If you focus on the browns, that's your reality; it's brown, it's dull, it's dark. If you focus on the colour in your life, so to speak, your life becomes colourful, bright and attractive. You are guaranteed to physically feel different when focusing on all the rich, beautiful colour in your life than when focusing on the dull, brown stuff. The choice is yours to make every single day.

Only *you* can direct the focus of your thoughts. Your mindset will shape your life, as thoughts ultimately influence our actions, habits, character and destiny:

- Your thoughts become words.

- Your words become actions.

- Your actions become habits.

- Your habits become character.

- Your character becomes your destiny.

That's profoundly simple and simply profound. Pay close attention to your thoughts if you want to positively impact your destiny.

Six mindsets to liberate your greatness

1. **Beginner's mindset** – Approach every situation with an open mind and without any preconceptions, eager to learn and grow while embracing curiosity and humility.

2. **Growth mindset** – Embrace challenges and see setbacks as opportunities for improvement. Carol Dweck is a renowned psychologist and professor at Stanford University, best known

for her groundbreaking research on mindset, motivation and personal development. In her book, *Mindset*, she said, 'In a growth mindset, challenges are exciting rather than threatening. So rather than thinking, "Oh, I'm going to reveal my weaknesses," you say, "Wow, here's a chance to grow."'[9]

3. **CEO mindset** – Take responsibility for your decisions, actions and results, leading with purpose and vision.

4. **Solution-oriented mindset** – Tackle challenges head-on, actively seeking and implementing solutions instead of dwelling on problems. Albert Einstein said, 'It's not that I'm so smart. I just stay with problems longer.'[10] His approach to problem solving was not to dwell on the problem in a way that created despair, but rather to spend quality time understanding it so he could find the solution. This mindset requires stamina and resilience. The more time and focus you give to understanding and solving a problem, the more obvious the solution becomes.

5. **Abundance mindset** – Focus on the limitless possibilities and opportunities, believing in the potential for success and fulfilment. Daniel Priestley, an entrepreneur, author and one of my close mentors, said to me in a conversation once, 'Someone has woken up today with the resources you need to succeed; you just need to find them.' I love the connection between people with resources and people with needs. If we all acknowledge that opportunity daily with the

courage to ask and to give, we'd be solving so
many more problems in the world.

6. **The ultimate soldier's mindset** – In Ant
   Middleton's bestselling book *Mental Fitness*, he
   says that 'Your body gets you to the battlefield,
   but it's your mind that wins the fight.'[11] Ant is
   a highly accomplished soldier, adventurer and
   leader who recognises the value of a strong,
   positive mindset. I can't even begin to imagine
   what it's like to be in a real-life war or on a
   battlefield, but I can fully appreciate how essential
   mindset is to survival on the battlefield of life and
   business. Condition your mind for mental fitness,
   so that you're able to face challenges head-on,
   survive and thrive in any environment.

A greater skillset

Equipped with a better mindset, greatness requires a
larger skillset. If you have a greatness mindset, I know
you know that to have more, achieve more and contribute more you first need to *become* more. If that's you, I
admire and applaud you for your decision to invest in
your personal and professional development.

When you hit a plateau and feel like you're stagnating, that's your opportunity to level up your skills.
Read a book, listen to a podcast, watch a YouTube
video, take an online course, join a mastermind, hire a
coach… do something to gain new insights and inspiration that could spark something inside of you to
accelerate your growth. When you learn faster, you'll
grow faster. As you make progress towards your goals,
you'll gain greater confidence and momentum.

Upskilling is critical for personal and professional development. It's about becoming the person you need to be to do the thing you want to do. In Chapter 3, we'll explore how to identify and proactively close gaps in your skillset by acquiring new skills.

Embrace the opportunity to learn and grow. It's the journey, the climb and the struggle that shapes your character and teaches you. The important message of Marie Forleo's book *Everything Is Figureoutable* is in the title.[12] That doesn't mean it's easy or comfortable, but it does mean that if you're committed to finding a way to win, you will succeed. Especially in today's world where we have access to all the information we need to succeed – the gurus, the strategies, the tools and the tactics... and, yes, AI too – everything is indeed figureoutable.

The more knowledge you acquire, the more knowledge you'll realise that you still need to acquire. Greek philosopher Socrates is said to have stated, 'I know that I am intelligent because I know that I know nothing.'[13] Intellectual humility and the recognition that there is always more knowledge to be gained is a gift you give to yourself and the people around you. Embrace the journey of acquiring and sharing knowledge.

A greater toolset

Now that you're equipped with a greater mindset and a formidable skillset, let's talk about the need for a more sophisticated toolset. Greatness demands that we become adept in using the right tools for the task at hand. There are countless ways to achieve your goals, but depending on the tools you choose, the journey could be expedited or drawn out.

Our world is filled with a myriad of tools designed to enhance our efficiency and effectiveness, from technology that automates mundane tasks to analytical software that interprets complex data. These tools, when used wisely, can be game-changers. The trick lies in discerning which tools are best suited for your objectives. Remember, the most advanced tool is only as good as the person using it. Mastery of your chosen tools is key.

As with your skillset, it's important to continually refine your toolset. The technological landscape is constantly evolving, so staying up-to-date with new advancements can ensure you remain on the cutting edge of your field. Don't be intimidated by new technologies; instead, embrace them as opportunities to increase your effectiveness and efficiency.

Choosing the right tools also requires a good deal of self-awareness. Understanding your strengths, weaknesses and work style can help you select tools that complement your abilities. The right tool can enhance your strengths, offset your weaknesses and seamlessly integrate into your work habits.

In essence, your journey to greatness is facilitated by a three-pronged approach: cultivating a greater mindset, developing a greater skillset and harnessing a greater toolset. These elements work in tandem on your quest towards personal mastery and professional excellence. Remember, with the right mindset, skillset and toolset, your potential is limitless.

Mastery and transformation take time

How do you master any skill? Malcolm Gladwell, in his book, *Outliers*,[14] popularised the idea that it takes approximately 10,000 hours of deliberate practice to achieve mastery in a particular field or skill. The concept is based on research conducted by psychologist K. Anders Ericsson, who studied the practice habits of experts in various fields such as music, sports and chess.[15] Mastery takes time. Transformation takes time.

When I ask my children, 'How do you master any skill?' Instinctively now they tell me, 'Study and practice!' Whenever they come up against an obstacle, that's what I encourage them to do.

As a family, we enjoy Spartan obstacle course racing. We love the positive vibe and energy of the events, being part of the fun Spartan culture, the exhilarating thrill of the obstacles and trails, and just being outdoors getting muddy! Personally, I appreciate the lessons the children learn as they figure out how to go over, under, around or through the obstacles. On my own health and well-being journey, the thing I see and value the most about our Spartan events is the journey to the starting line, and recognising that everyone has had to overcome so many obstacles just to get there.

Whatever skill you're trying to acquire or craft you're striving to master, study the principles, methodology, theory, habits and successes of those who've achieved what you want to achieve. Then put your new-found knowledge into practice.

If the key to mastery is study and practice, and you genuinely believe in continual improvement, you could use the following steps:

- Know what you want to achieve.
- Study the information available.

- Practise what you've learnt by applying the information.

- Study the results you're getting.

- Study more effective and efficient ways for achieving your desired outcome.

- Practise with new insights, applying the nuances you've now learnt.

- Study the results you're getting.

- Practise fine-tuning, while you test, learn and iterate.

- Rinse and repeat.

Mastery is not about doing 10,000 things; it's about doing a few things 10,000 times. Bruce Lee, the famous martial artist, and actor, once said, 'I fear not the man who has practised 10,000 kicks once, but I fear the man who has practised one kick 10,000 times.'[16] A powerful insight. That level of mastery comes through study and repeated, focused practice, rather than trying to learn many different skills without truly mastering any of them.

Bruce Lee's approach to mastery

Bruce Lee was celebrated not only for his exceptional physical abilities but also for his distinctive approach and viewpoint on mastery. He considered himself a perpetual student of martial arts – continuously learning and enhancing his skills – rather than a master who had attained the apex of his art.

Bruce Lee's expertise in martial arts stemmed from his unwavering commitment to training, exploration and experimentation with various methods and philosophies throughout his life. Rooted in fluidity, adaptation and self-discovery, his teachings continue to inspire countless people – including me – across various disciplines.

Embracing fluidity

One of Bruce Lee's most famous quotes is, 'Be water, my friend.'[17] He believed that mastery came from being able to adapt and flow in any situation, just like water. Water is shapeless and formless, yet it can move around obstacles and even wear them down over time. By embracing fluidity, we learn to let go of rigid ideas and preconceived notions, allowing ourselves to be more responsive and flexible in any situation.

Adaptation and continuous learning

Bruce Lee was a lifelong learner who continually sought to refine his skills and knowledge. He believed that true mastery required constant adaptation and evolution, as stagnation would only lead to decay. By integrating different martial arts styles and techniques into his own unique approach, Lee demonstrated the importance of cross-disciplinary learning and open-mindedness in the pursuit of mastery.

Self-discovery and personal growth

For Bruce Lee, mastery was not just about technical proficiency but also about self-discovery and personal growth. He believed that the journey towards mastery should be an introspective one, where we delve deep into ourselves to uncover our strengths and weaknesses. Through self-awareness and self-reflection, we can develop a better understanding of our abilities and limitations, allowing us to push our boundaries and grow as individuals.

Applying Bruce Lee's philosophy

Bruce Lee's approach to mastery can be applied to various aspects of our lives, including business, personal development and relationships. By embracing fluidity, adaptation and self-discovery, we can develop a greater sense of self-awareness and resilience, which can lead to personal and professional growth (more on awareness in Chapter 3).

Study and practise without judgement but with a spirit of excellence and a desire to continually improve. Trust the process and enjoy the journey of becoming masterful in a particular field or skill because mastery and transformation take time.

Greatness requires consistent incremental improvements

Excellence is the gradual result of always striving to be better. My team know that if today my way is the best way of doing something, and they come up with a better way, then we do it their way because we strive to have a spirit of excellence. It's about continual improvement, having the humility to learn and grow and the desire to make things better – to be 1% better every day.

The Progress Principle is a brilliant book that reveals how small wins and incremental progress can lead to significant achievements and happiness.[18] Authors Teresa Amabile and Steven Kramer emphasise the importance of recognising and celebrating daily accomplishments to fuel motivation and foster a sense of fulfilment.

Sir Dave Brailsford, the former performance director of British Cycling, is often credited with popularising the principle of marginal gains.[19] This concept revolves around making small, incremental improvements in multiple areas, which when combined lead to significant overall progress. Brailsford believed that by focusing on achieving just a 1% improvement in various aspects of a task or process, the cumulative effect of these minor enhancements would result in a substantial positive impact. Under his leadership, this approach transformed British Cycling, leading to numerous successes and gold medals. The principle of marginal gains encourages individuals and organisations to identify opportunities for growth in every detail, fostering a culture of continuous improvement and long-term success.

Zappos, the online shoe and clothing retailer, also embraced a philosophy of continuous improvement by encouraging its employees to get 1% better every day.[20] This approach aimed to create a culture of constant learning and growth, where each team member focused on making small, incremental improvements in their skills, knowledge and performance. By fostering this mindset, Zappos believed that the cumulative effect of these daily improvements would lead to significant overall progress and success for both the individual employees and the company. This philosophy helped Zappos become renowned not only for its excellent customer service but also for its innovative and positive work culture.

Greatness requires a spirit of excellence

By taking a quick look at a list of the top companies in the world, including Apple, Amazon, Alphabet (Google), Disney, Microsoft, Tesla and others, you'll notice they constantly strive for excellence by focusing on innovation, customer service, quality, culture and continuous improvement in their respective industries.

In my coffee shop days, our team members who swept the floors and cleaned the restrooms had a higher spirit of excellence than some of the other restaurant managers in town. Excellence is not a role, a title, a position or a badge of honour. When I talk about excellence as part of a high-performing team's DNA, I'm emphasising that the quest for excellence is woven into the very fabric of the team's culture, values and mindset. It's not just a goal but an intrinsic trait that guides their decisions, actions and behaviours every single day.

A high-performing team that truly embraces excellence is endlessly committed to producing exceptional results, continuously refining their skills and setting the bar high for themselves and their work. They tackle challenges head-on, see setbacks as opportunities to learn and push the limits of what's possible. These teams cultivate an atmosphere of open communication, collaboration and co-creation, where each person is encouraged to take charge of their work, think outside the box, support each other and contribute their unique strengths and insights to achieve shared success.

Leaders of such teams are essential in nurturing this culture of excellence. They set clear expectations, exemplify the desired behaviours and provide the necessary resources, guidance and encouragement for team members to grow, innovate and excel. By celebrating victories, treating failures as priceless learning experiences and stressing the importance of continuous improvement, leaders can make sure that the pursuit of excellence remains at the heart of their team's DNA.

As a leader, how are you instilling a spirit of excellence within your team to drive growth and success?

Five practical steps to cultivate a spirit of excellence

1. **Encourage curiosity:** Foster an environment where asking questions is encouraged. Stimulate thought and inspire learning by posing thought-provoking questions and promoting open discussions.

2. **Enable learning:** Provide resources and opportunities for your team members to continually develop their skills and knowledge. Offer training, workshops and other learning experiences to help them achieve mastery.

3. **Empower people to take action:** Encourage team members to apply their newly acquired knowledge and skills in their work. Support them in taking the initiative and making decisions that align with your organisation's goals and values.

4. **Embed teaching and sharing:** Encourage your team members to teach and share their expertise with others. This not only helps others grow but

also reinforces the individual's understanding of the subject matter.

5. **Embody a coaching culture:** Lead by example and develop a culture where team members coach one another to improve and excel. This collaborative approach empowers everyone to reach their full potential and contribute to the team's overall success.

By managing and measuring your team's progress, you'll see continuous improvement. No matter what level your team is currently at, there's always another level of success and significance to achieve. Keep pushing the boundaries and striving for excellence together.

Six levels of mastery in personal and professional growth

1. Curiosity – asking questions with a sincere desire to explore

2. Learning something new

3. Applying your knowledge to develop your skills

4. Teaching others to increase their knowledge

5. Coaching others to develop their skills

6. Role modelling consistently for others to follow your example

I am passionate about learning and development, having created numerous corporate academies and training programmes. I could speak about these six levels of mastery for days!

How would you rate yourself in each of the six levels? What could you do to accelerate your personal and professional growth?

Excellence is never an accident; it comes with consistent work. Work smart, work hard and success will gravitate towards you when you do things with a spirit of excellence.

The SENSE Framework®

I have had the privilege of working with countless individuals on their personal and professional journeys. Over the years, I've observed that the most successful people share a common trait: they prioritise their well-being and understand the importance of a balanced lifestyle.

I also noticed that many people struggle to find harmony in their lives. In our pursuit of success, we often sacrifice the very things that keep us grounded, healthy and energised. This observation inspired me to create a simple yet powerful framework, designed to help individuals regain control over their lives and achieve lasting success.

Whenever I facilitated sales, marketing and leadership development workshops around the world, I found myself compelled to encourage delegates to eat healthier, work out more often, be more intentional about their sleep and so on. I truly believe that mastering personal habits is essential for personal and professional progress. It's a must, not a 'nice to have'.

The SENSE Framework is the culmination of years of research, experience and collaboration with experts across various fields. It is based on the core belief that holistic well-being is the foundation for personal and professional growth. Each letter in the acronym represents a crucial aspect of our lives: sleep, exercise, nutrition, spirit and environment. By focusing on these five core pillars, we can create a balanced foundation for personal and professional growth, empowering us to reach our full potential.

Sleep

Sleep is essential for maintaining optimal cognitive function, emotional regulation and physical health. It allows our bodies and minds to recover and recharge, preparing us for the challenges that lie ahead.

Tips for improvement

- **Stick to a sleep schedule** – Going to bed and waking up at the same time every day can help regulate your body's internal clock.

- **Create a restful environment** – Ensure your bedroom is dark, quiet and cool. Consider using room-darkening shades, earplugs or other devices to create an environment conducive to sleep.

- **Limit screen time at least an hour before bed** – The light emitted by phones, computers and TVs can interfere with the production of the sleep hormone melatonin.

- **Duration and quality is key** – Aim for seven to nine hours of sleep per night of 85%+ quality.

Exercise

Regular physical activity has numerous physical and mental health benefits, including improved mood, increased energy levels and reduced risk of chronic health issues. Exercise also helps to manage stress and enhance overall well-being.

Tips for improvement

- **Incorporate exercise into your daily routine** – Try to get at least thirty minutes of moderate physical activity most days of the week.

- **Mix it up** – Variety keeps your workouts interesting and helps to work different muscle groups.

- **Listen to your body** – If you feel pain, shortness of breath, dizziness or nausea, take a break or slow down.

- **Rest** – Take a rest day every three to four days to let your muscles recover.

Nutrition

A balanced diet is crucial for providing our bodies with the necessary fuel to function effectively. Proper nutrition contributes to optimal physical and mental performance and supports our long-term health.

Tips for improvement

- **Eat a variety of foods** – This ensures that you get a wide range of nutrients your body needs to function properly.

- **Stay hydrated** – Water plays a critical role in every function of the body.

- **Limit processed foods and sugars** – These often contain empty calories and lack the nutrients your body needs.

- **Go hard on the plan and easy on yourself** – Aim to get your nutrition 80% right. It's OK to have a treat now and then, as long as you make the next meal a healthy choice.

Spirit

The spirit pillar refers to our inner life, encompassing faith, mindfulness, purpose and emotional resilience. By cultivating a strong sense of spirit, we can better navigate the ups and downs of life, maintain a positive outlook and stay connected to our true selves.

Tips for improvement

- **Start your day with quiet time** – Be still, give thanks for a new day and all the opportunities you have to make a positive impact in the world.

- **Live in an attitude of gratitude** – Make a habit of recognising and appreciating everything you already have in your life.

- **Practise mindfulness** – Engage in activities that help you stay present and focused.

- **Foster connections** – Build and maintain strong relationships with people who support and inspire you.

Environment

Our surroundings have a significant impact on our overall well-being, productivity and success. By creating a supportive and nurturing environment, we can foster personal and professional growth, allowing us to thrive.

Tips for improvement

- **Organise your space** – A clean, orderly environment can increase focus and productivity.

- **Bring nature indoors** – Plants can purify the air and boost mood and creativity.

- **Control noise** – Use noise-cancelling headphones or instrumental music if you need to concentrate in a noisy environment.

- **Get outdoors into the environment** – Blue skies, fresh air and nature is guaranteed to energise you.

Make common SENSE common practice

The idea behind the SENSE Framework is not to introduce groundbreaking new concepts but rather to remind us of the fundamental principles that we often overlook in our busy lives. Make common SENSE common practice and you will unlock the keys to sustainable success and happiness.

People who prioritise their well-being are better equipped to handle stress, make thoughtful decisions and maintain healthy relationships, both in their personal and professional lives. When we neglect our well-being, we may experience burnout, reduced productivity and even physical and mental health issues. It's essential to recognise that success is not merely about achieving external milestones; it also encompasses our internal state of well-being.

If you'd like to go deeper on improving your SENSE, take the SENSE scorecard at www.sense-scorecard.com. You'll receive a personalised report, and I'll send you my e-book, entitled *Make Common SENSE Common Practice*.

Trust me and trust the process. If you make common SENSE common practice, you will be able to generate energy on demand – and that will become a superpower for you as you set out to liberate your greatness.

Take time to reflect and refocus

Reflection is a skill that holds immense value in both our personal and professional lives. Because it requires us to spend a little time and attention, it's often overlooked and neglected. If you invest time in developing reflection as a skill, this powerful practice will enable you to delve deeper into your experiences, learning and decision-making processes, facilitating even more personal growth and development.

By cultivating the skill of reflection as part of your daily routine, you will gain insights, identify patterns and uncover opportunities for improvement, ultimately leading to a heightened sense of self-awareness and enhanced effectiveness in various aspects of your life. That's a brilliant return on your time invested. To help, I've built in reflection time for you at the end of every chapter.

As you read through this book, challenge yourself to look for new insights, spend time reflecting on your current knowledge, beliefs, feelings and actions, and question:

- What can I do to go to my next level of success and significance?

- How can I apply the principles to accelerate my growth, achieve my goals faster and amplify my results?

- How can I inspire others to come on that journey with me?

If your attitude determines your altitude, with the right attitude there's another level for you to achieve!

Think about some of the most inspiring people you've worked with. How would you rate them on skill and attitude? The most inspiring people may not have had the most skill, but guaranteed they had the best attitudes.

Skill can be taught; attitude must be caught. In fact, you can feel someone's attitude regardless of the words they're using. A positive can-do, let's-make-this-happen-together attitude is positively infectious.

Summary

It is crucial to remember that your growth is ultimately your own responsibility. By taking ownership of your personal and professional development, you can unlock your full potential and pave the way for a future filled with success, significance and the ability to make a positive lasting impact in the world around you.

The journey to liberating your greatness begins with the understanding that your growth is your business. By continually investing in yourself, seeking new opportunities for learning, taking the time to reflect and improve, and embracing a mindset of continuous improvement, along with patience to master your skills and a spirit of excellence, you are fostering the conditions necessary for achieving personal mastery and professional excellence. In doing so, you are not only setting yourself up for a life of greatness but also inspiring those around you to do the same.

The pursuit of personal mastery and professional excellence is a lifelong journey – one that will undoubtedly lead to a life of fulfilment, purpose and the realisation of your greatest dreams. Embrace the challenge, take ownership of your growth and begin the incredible journey towards liberating your greatness.

Practical application

Reflect on personal mastery and professional excellence

Reflection is a skill. Take a moment to capture your thoughts and commit to taking consistent action to move the needle forward:

- What key insights did you discover in this chapter?

- What decisions are you committed to making to gain the greatest return?

- What disciplined action will you take in the next week/month/quarter that will give you the greatest reward?

Activity

In the spirit of striving for excellence and continual improvement, what will you...

STOP
(Doing / thinking
/ believing / feeling)

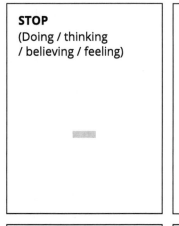

START
(Doing / thinking
/ believing / feeling)

CONTINUE
(Doing / thinking
/ believing / feeling)

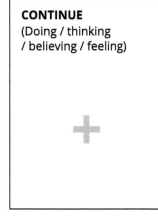

LEARN
(Book / online course
/ audio)

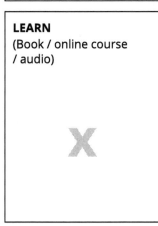

PART TWO

INSIGHT

In this second part of *Liberate Your Greatness*, we'll delve into the transformative power of awareness and alignment. Gaining insight into yourself, others and your surroundings is the foundation for personal and professional growth.

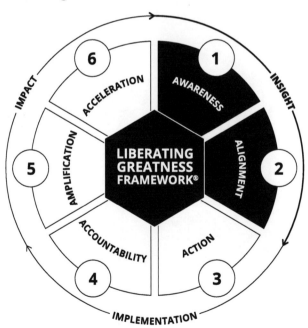

This section will equip you with the tools to cultivate greater awareness, recognise opportunities and understand the importance of aligning your vision, purpose, mission, values and people. As you embark on this journey of self-discovery and reflection, you'll begin to unlock your true potential and pave the way for a life of greatness.

Embrace the insights presented in Part Two and let them guide you towards a deeper understanding of your strengths, passions and aspirations. By doing so, you'll not only learn how to recognise your unique gifts but also how to align them with your goals and objectives.

The insights offered in this section will serve as a catalyst for change, inspiring you to create a life of fulfilment, purpose and success at work and at home. When you have great awareness and alignment, you'll implement your plans with laser focus. Clarity brings peace – that's the power of insight.

THREE

The Principle Of Awareness

All proactive change starts with awareness

The Principle of Awareness is the foundation upon which your journey to greatness begins. In this chapter, we'll explore the importance of self-awareness and its role in fostering personal growth and professional success. By developing a deep understanding of your strengths, weaknesses, values and motivations, you'll be better equipped to identify opportunities for improvement and make informed decisions that align with your ultimate vision for your life and career.

Strive for greater clarity, confidence, courage and competence

Liberating your greatness requires a commitment to moving from where you are to where you want to be, with the confidence to figure things out along the way and the courage to step out of your comfort zone and take consistent action.

Awareness, by definition, is 'having knowledge or perception of a situation or fact'.[21] It's heightened consciousness. It's often a revelation that something needs to change, even though you may not know exactly what needs to change or how to achieve the desired outcome. Awareness is a crucial aspect of personal and professional development. It is the ability to understand and recognise one's own emotions, thoughts and beliefs, as well as those of others. Being aware allows individuals to make informed decisions, communicate effectively and build strong relationships.

In the business world, your awareness can have a significant impact on your success. By understanding your own strengths and weaknesses, you can identify areas for improvement and work on developing the skills you need to excel in your career. Heightened awareness also allows you to recognise opportunities and challenges in the business environment, enabling you to make strategic decisions and adapt to changing circumstances.

Over the past two decades, I've had the privilege of building sales and marketing academies for global and local FMCG (fast-moving consumer goods) companies. I've also coached and trained entrepreneurs and senior executive leaders, along with their teams, in thirty-three countries around the world. The primary objective for all the academies and coaching my team and I deliver is to develop the personal and professional capability of individuals and teams by helping them improve their knowledge, confidence and competence. Part of that journey is acknowledging the current reality and desired future reality, identifying the gap and then determining how to close or bridge that gap.

The confidence–competence loop

In psychology, the confidence–competence loop describes how confidence increases when competence increases. It stands to reason that the more competent you are, the better your ability, knowledge or skill to do something successfully, and therefore the more confident you'll feel when doing it. Most people believe they must be competent first to then have the confidence to take action.

Have you ever been in that situation where you hold back because you feel you're not quite competent enough to step forward? Well, the beautiful thing about the confidence–competence loop is that it's an infinity loop for a reason. You don't have to start with competence; you can start with confidence.

When you're experiencing imposter syndrome – feeling like you're not yet competent enough in a particular area of your personal or professional life – have the confidence to start, to take bold, courageous action, with the humility to test, learn, fail forward and grow. As you do multiple repetitions you will develop more competence in that area, which in turn leads to even more confidence!

Renowned speaker Zig Ziglar said, 'You don't have to be great to start, but you have to start to be great.'[22] My recommendation is for you to start with confidence, even before you're competent.

Ignorance is not bliss – it's costly

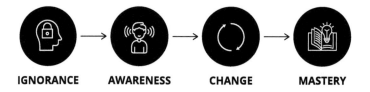

IGNORANCE   AWARENESS   CHANGE   MASTERY

In learning and capability development, we often refer to ignorance as a state of 'unconscious incompetence'. If you're unconsciously incompetent, you're unaware of your lack of competence in a particular area. You could potentially live in ignorance forever, or until you gain greater awareness. Without the right level of awareness, information and insights, you could make serious, costly mistakes in life and in business.

When you don't know what you don't know, where do you even begin to make positive shifts in the right direction? A great place to start is awareness. Proactive change can only happen after you become aware of where you are now and where you want to be.

The gap highlights the difference between your current reality and desired future reality. It shows you what you want to move away from and move towards. Your awareness of your gap will motivate you to take action because of either inspiration or desperation. Do you want to move towards pleasure, a bigger prize or a greater payoff? Or do you want to move away from pain or the current problems you're facing?

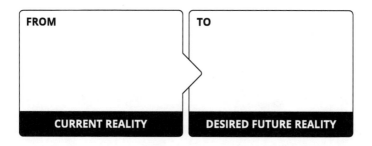

Awareness is the first step to mastery. Any journey of mastery starts with being aware of where you are now, where you want to go and what you need to do to get there.

Where do you want to go from or to?

Here are some practical questions to ask when assessing your current reality and desired future reality – and exploring options for how to close or bridge the gap:

- What's your current reality?

- What's your desired future reality?

- What's the central question you're trying to answer?

- What problem are you trying to solve?

- What are the gaps and how will you close them?

- What options do you have?

- What questions should you be asking that you're not yet asking?

- What do you need to do differently?

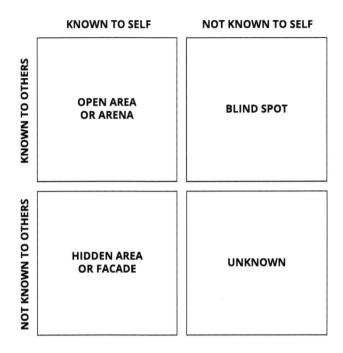

The Johari window is a psychological tool that was created by Joseph Luft and Harrington Ingham in 1955 to help individuals better understand their relationships with themselves and others.[23] It is designed to enhance self-awareness, communication and interpersonal relationships. The model consists of four quadrants (or 'windows') that represent different aspects of an individual's personality:

- **Open area or arena:** This quadrant represents traits, behaviours and information that both the individual and others are aware of. It is the shared knowledge between a person and their peers.

- **Blind spot:** This quadrant represents traits and behaviours that others can observe but the individual is unaware of. These are aspects that can be revealed through feedback from others.

- **Hidden area or façade:** This quadrant includes information that the individual knows about themselves but has not revealed to others. This can be due to a desire for privacy or a fear of vulnerability.

- **Unknown:** This quadrant contains information that is unknown to both the individual and to others. It can include undiscovered talents, unconscious biases or repressed feelings.

By using the Johari window, individuals can work towards increasing their self-awareness and improving their communication and relationships with others. This is achieved by expanding the open area through self-disclosure and receiving feedback, which helps to reduce the hidden and blind areas.

Not many people like receiving feedback for fear of embarrassment or a knock to their confidence. But, if I was presenting to you and your leadership team in a boardroom after lunch and I had spinach in my teeth, trust me, I would want you to tell me. Rather than you being distracted by it for the whole session and me looking like a fool, I'd want the feedback!

Leaders and followers often have blind spots that others are aware of but which they aren't. By proactively requesting and embracing feedback, in the spirit of learning and growing, you can create more open areas with your team, which unlocks greater communication and collaboration. You'll be able to tap into each other's strengths better and therefore accelerate your progress.

I remember a brutally defining moment of self-awareness in my mid-thirties at a golf day that I once hosted. After I finished facilitating the prize-giving, I walked around the room greeting guests, cracking jokes and thanking them for their participation and support. I then bumped into someone whom I hadn't seen since the previous year's golf day. I put out my hand to shake his, and instead of grabbing my hand, he grabbed the side of my waist and said, 'Have you put all this weight on in one year? If you carry on the way you're going, next year you'll look like that guy, and the following year you'll look like that guy.' He pointed to two fairly large, older gentlemen, well beyond their prime.

My first thought was, 'I'm never inviting him to a golf day again. How rude! How insensitive he was to the fact that I now have three children, life and work is busy and I like food!' Then it hit me. How true. He was right. I hadn't done any sort of exercise for months. I'd picked up bad eating and sleeping habits and had gradually drifted so far off track with my health… and I hadn't even realised it. I was ignorant of my current reality until my friend helped me gain the much-needed self-awareness required to shock me into action. What a gift he gave me.

That moment of awareness was a pivotal shift in my well-being that forced me to face my current reality and decide to focus on my personal health and fitness. I'm now so grateful for his brutal honesty, which turned out to be one of the kindest gestures.

You can't fix what you won't face

Awareness is an important step in your journey to change. The fact that you're aware of a gap, a development area or something that needs to improve means you've already started the process of becoming better.

You take ownership of the fact that *you* need to change if you want to change the situation.

In my personal story above, I literally had to stand in front of the mirror, and on the scale, accept my current reality and decide to change. You can improve any area of your life and business when you're clear on your current reality, clear on your goal or desired future reality and have a plan that you can implement.

Are you potentially missing out on opportunities you don't know exist right in front of you? In your personal life, you could do a self-assessment, personality profile, strength assessment or one of our high-performance individual or team scorecards. There are so many wonderful ways of increasing your awareness about who you are, how you're showing up, who you want to become and where you need to focus your time, energy and effort to go to your next level.

At work, you could get feedback from your peers or guidance from a coach. You could proactively ask others for their perspective on how they think you're doing. What's working well? What could be even better? Be open to what they share with you. Be professionally curious about the insights you discover.

Gaining candid feedback

I recognise you might be afraid of asking for feedback, so I want to encourage you to embrace the opportunity to learn and grow. Here's a practical approach of soliciting feedback and asking for input:

I'm focused on my personal and professional development, and I would value your input.

I'm impossible to offend, and keen to learn and grow, so please share your true, authentic perspective. What are some things you feel I'm doing well? What areas would be even better if I did something differently?

When you frame feedback as an opportunity for others to help you on your personal and professional development journey, they will most likely lean in, be kind and candid, and provide you with incredibly valuable insights that will fast track your success.

Lead by example

From an organisational point of view, what sort of culture are you striving to achieve? What you tolerate, you permit. By tolerating certain behaviours or attitudes, you implicitly give permission for those behaviours to continue, reinforcing their acceptability within your team or organisation. The culture in your business will be determined by your awareness, alignment and actions. Will you lead by example or be an example of how *not* to lead?

I left the corporate world because I was tired of listening to stories about people being taken apart in public in presentations to senior leaders. I'm all for being candid, but I think you can be kind and candid without being direct and destructive. Toxic behaviour from senior leaders creates a toxic culture that permeates through the entire organisation, which will take years of intentional transformation to overcome.

You'll ultimately need to replace all the leaders responsible for toxic behaviour, as well as those that stood by and let it happen. It's why I'm so passionate about helping visionary leaders and entrepreneurs transform their businesses by creating a culture of high performance, while maintaining well-being and positive relationships.

Not saying anything says a lot. You can't fix what you won't face, so choose to face it, fix it, and create a positive and productive culture.

Minor tweaks can have major impact

Your mindset plays an important role in whether your heightened self-awareness holds you back or propels you forward. Do you get defensive or deflated when you receive feedback, or do you become excited about the insights you've learnt that can help you raise your game?

Think like an athlete

Athletes know that feedback is a gift. They crave it. In fact, they demand it. They know that minor tweaks can have a major impact. One small adjustment in technique could be the deciding factor between first and second place.

Athletes proactively ask for perspective. They analyse data for insights that help them learn, grow and improve their mindset, skillset and toolset. They view feedback as an opportunity to get better.

Kobe Bryant, one of basketball's greatest players of all time, often spoke about his constant quest for trying to be better every day. His approach was to practise, to train as much and as often as he could, and to always ask questions. How could he improve? What would he need to do to become the best player he could be? He explained, 'I call people all the time. If I want to learn something, I pick up the phone and ask.'[24]

He had the humility to recognise that others could help him fast track his success by providing insight, perspective and feedback. He also had the drive to study and practise, which, as we discussed earlier, is the key to mastering any skill.

Perspective is powerful

If you're playing any sport, your perspective of what you're doing is different to that of a coach who's looking at you from a different angle. Take golf as an example: if you're looking down at the ball with the club in your hand, getting ready to hit it, your perspective is different to your coach's, who will see things you're not seeing. They may observe that you're leaning too far forward or too far back; they may notice your club face being slightly open or closed. Helping you identify areas for improvement to minor tweaks makes a major difference 300 yards down the line!

Three areas to gain greater awareness

There are three areas of awareness that will accelerate your growth, achieve your goals faster and amplify your impact:

1. Awareness of self/self-awareness

2. Awareness of others

3. Awareness of dependence, independence and interdependence

Let's look at each of these.

Awareness of self/self-awareness

Every journey of self-mastery begins with self-awareness of where you are now, where you want to be, what you need to do and who you need to become to achieve your goals. It's impossible to grow without self-awareness.

The *Oxford English Dictionary* defines self-awareness as: 'Conscious knowledge of one's own character'[25] and character as: 'All the qualities and features that make a person, groups of people, and places different from others' (your thoughts, feelings, motives and desires).[26]

Socrates is known to have said something to the effect of, 'To know thyself is the beginning of wisdom.'[27] What an incredible gift to yourself – and everyone around you – when you take a moment to pause, reflect, observe your thoughts, feelings, motives and desires, and get to know yourself better. That's how to internalise your wins and take note of the lessons you're learning as you fail forward in other areas of your life. Failing forward happens when you embrace opportunities to test, fail, learn and grow without judgement. Often one of the biggest benefits of receiving coaching is gaining new perspective that increases your self-awareness. Coaches help you to gain awareness of where you are now, to identify strengths and areas of improvement and to create an even bigger vision for your best future self.

In a world with so much uncertainty and so many things you can't control, you can always take charge of your thoughts, feelings, motives and desires. You can control your words and actions too, by choosing how to respond to these.

Have you ever been in a situation where you've had a negative thought that made you feel deflated? It's OK to have negative thoughts – we all have them from time to time. What do you do with them, though? Do you allow them to take you down a negative spiral, where the negative thought leads to you feeling deflated, discouraged, demotivated, doubtful and depressed? Or do you catch those thoughts and say, 'I see you, negative thought! I feel you. But I'm not going to let you take me down that negative spiral.' Instead, you redirect your mind and ask yourself, 'What's one positive thing I can do? What's in my control: my thoughts, words and actions.'

You can always choose how long you allow yourself to dwell on negative thoughts. Will you choose prolonged self-pity; beating yourself up repeatedly, which has absolutely zero productive benefit? Or will you choose to learn from the situation, say to yourself without judgement, 'It is what it is', then embrace the struggle and opportunity to grow and pivot quickly to your next level?

When you start taking positive action you begin a positive upward spiral of solution-oriented, future-focused thoughts and actions. As you regain momentum through a series of small, positive steps in the right direction, it allows you to bounce back quickly and avoid dwelling on negative thoughts and feelings.

Personality profiling tools

There are several personality profiling tools that can help you enhance your self-awareness and gain insights into your strengths, weaknesses and preferences. Use these tools and insights to understand why you do what you do, and why those around you think and behave the way they do too. Some of the most popular and widely used tools include:

- **Myers-Briggs Type Indicator® (MBTI®)** – The MBTI assessment builds a strong foundation for lifelong personal development by defining personality types.[28] It gives a constructive, flexible and liberating framework for understanding individual differences and strengths. The MBTI personality assessment tool indicates your personality preferences in four dimensions:

  — Where you focus your attention: extraversion (E) or introversion (I)

  — The way you take in information: sensing (S) or iNtuition (N)

  — How you make decisions: thinking (T) or feeling (F)

  — How you deal with the world: judging (J) or perceiving (P)

  The four letters that make up your personality type can help you to understand yourself and your interactions with others.

- **DiSC® Assessment** – DiSC® is an acronym that stands for the four main behavioural styles outlined in the DiSC model of personalities:

dominance, influence, steadiness and conscientiousness.[29] It helps leaders understand their communication style, decision-making approach and how they interact with others in a team or work environment. According to discprofile.com, 'DiSC® simply helps us find out which style we tend to gravitate towards most – our comfort zone. With that knowledge, we can understand our underlying tendencies and preferences and adapt our behaviours to interact with others more effectively.'

- **CliftonStrengths®** – Invented by Don Clifton, this assessment uncovers your unique rank order of thirty-four CliftonStrengths themes, which explain how you most naturally think, feel and behave. Gallup's research shows that people who know and use their CliftonStrengths are more engaged at work, more productive in their roles, happier and healthier.[30]

  I personally found it incredibly liberating when I first discovered my top five innate talents through the CliftonStrengths assessment. It helped me to understand why I think and behave in a particular way and to realise that I don't need to develop strengths in all thirty-four themes. Instead, I learnt to collaborate with those who have the relevant strengths I require to establish a successful team or project.

- **Enneagram Type Descriptions** – The Enneagram Institute® has a personality typing system that categorises people into nine distinct types (the reformer, helper, achiever, individualist, investigator, loyalist, enthusiast, challenger and peacemaker), each with its own set of motivations, fears and desires.[31] Understanding your Enneagram type can provide valuable insights into personal growth and relationships.

Whichever of the personality profiling tools you decide to explore, remember that they provide a lens through which you can view yourself and others. They're not to be used as predictors of the future and should be kept in the context of clarity and understanding, rather than any form of conclusive judgement.

If you want to increase your self-awareness without taking a personality assessment, ask yourself the following questions:

- Who am I?

- What roles do I play?

- What values, beliefs and priorities guide my life?

- How aware am I of my strengths and areas for improvement?

- Am I aware of my emotions and how they influence my thoughts and actions?

- How do I bounce back from setbacks and challenges?

- Do I reflect and learn from my experiences?

- How often do I seek feedback to uncover my blind spots?

- Am I open to growth, even when uncomfortable?

- Do my actions align with my values and goals?

- Do I take responsibility for my decisions and their consequences, both positive and negative?

- How well do I manage stress and work-life balance?

- What dreams and goals fuel my ambitions?

- Who do I need to become to achieve my dreams?

- What skills must I develop for success?

- Where is my attention and energy directed?

- Where am I on my journey from survival to success to significance?

Which questions sparked interest and resonated with you? You may have additional positive, empowering questions you could ask yourself. By asking yourself questions and reflecting on your answers, you will gain a deeper understanding of yourself, your motivations and your behaviours. This increased self-awareness will empower you to make more informed choices, better manage your emotions, and enhance your personal and professional growth.

Greater self-awareness leads to greater appreciation, self-acceptance and grace for your current reality, which in turn leads to greater action, self-accountability, self-mastery and impact. Now that's a positive spiral! It also demonstrates your humility to accept things the way they are, and demonstrates your passion to learn, grow and make them better than they are today.

Awareness of others

Succeeding socially and professionally depends on your ability to connect and build relationships with others. Demonstrating empathy, seeking clarity and understanding others' frames of reference, feelings, motivations and drivers increases our awareness of them and helps us connect in a more meaningful way.

One of the senior executives I coach has this really dialled in. He has remarkable self-awareness and awareness of others. He is thoughtful about the individuals and teams he engages with and intentionally seeks to understand who they really are and what their needs, concerns, challenges and opportunities are. He asks great questions and listens because he genuinely wants to hear their thoughts. People feel seen, heard and valued by him, and as a result they respect, admire and appreciate his leadership. He's a wonderful role model throughout the organisation.

Embracing diversity

Expanding your awareness of others is not only essential for fostering strong connections and relationships but also for embracing the full spectrum of diversity that exists in our world. Beyond the commonly discussed aspects of diversity, such as race, ethnicity, gender and sexual orientation, there are several other dimensions to consider. These include age, socio-economic background, education, religion and even differing abilities.

By demonstrating empathy and embracing cognitive diversity, you're acknowledging and appreciating the wealth of unique perspectives and experiences that everyone brings to the table. This broader understanding of diversity fosters an inclusive environment where people feel seen, heard and valued for who they are. As you cultivate your awareness of others and nurture a diverse and inclusive mindset, you'll unlock the potential for increased creativity, innovation and problem solving within your teams and organisations.

Embracing diversity also leads to increased employee satisfaction, higher levels of engagement and a greater sense of belonging, ultimately contributing to the overall success and growth of your organisation.

So, as you continue your journey of personal mastery and professional excellence, remember to prioritise your awareness of others and embrace the rich tapestry of diversity that surrounds you. Doing so will not only elevate your leadership skills but also create a positive and lasting impact on those you serve and the communities in which you live and work.

Increasing awareness to enhance your relationships

Business is – and always will be – about people dealing with people. So, what can you do to increase your awareness of others so that you can enhance your relationships?

If you want to increase your awareness of others, ask your yourself these questions:

- How present am I for the people in my life?

- Do I truly know those around me; their needs, dreams and challenges?

- Am I genuinely curious about others' experiences and perspectives?

- Do I actively listen and create safe spaces for open discussions?

- How aware am I of my biases and assumptions when perceiving others?

- Can I adapt my communication style to connect with diverse individuals?

- Do I seek opportunities to engage with people different from me?

- How can I show more empathy and support for those facing challenges?

Awareness of others requires consideration, empathy and compassion. Reflecting on these questions and considering the answers will help you increase your awareness of others, improve your understanding of the diverse individuals you encounter, and ultimately strengthen your relationships and leadership skills.

Greater awareness of others leads to greater empathy, communication, opportunities to collaborate, connection and trust. All relationships are built on trust. It starts with you genuinely increasing your awareness of others.

Awareness of dependence, independence and interdependence

With great self-awareness and enhanced awareness of others, I'd encourage you to analyse the situation you're in, so that you're able to explore potential synergies.

Stephen R Covey's concept of the maturity continuum is primarily discussed in his bestselling book, *The 7 Habits of Highly Effective People*.[32] Here, Covey introduces the idea of the stages of maturity as moving from dependence to independence (self-mastery and self-reliance) and finally to interdependence (collaborating and succeeding with others).

The Situational Leadership model featured in *Leadership and the One Minute Manager*,[33] identifies four development levels that describe the stages people progress through as they move from dependence to independence (from enthusiastic beginner, to disillusioned learner, to capable but cautious performer and then finally to self-reliant achiever). In this model, Ken Blanchard emphasises that leaders should adapt their leadership style based on the development level of the individuals they lead, so they can more effectively support their team members' growth and development. Based on the team members' development levels, leaders should adapt their leadership styles from *directing* enthusiastic beginners, to *coaching* disillusioned learners, to *supporting* capable but cautious performers, and then finally *delegating to* self-reliant achievers.

Progressing beyond independence – when you become more aware of your own and others' strengths and limitations – you'll identify opportunities for interdependence. You may also realise that you need to be even more dependent on others. While that might seem like going backwards on the maturity continuum, I'd like to argue that it's a step beyond interdependence, when you have the strength and courage to recognise that you are dependent on others too. If you're religious, that could mean you're dependent on God for daily blessing, protection, provision, favour, love, mercy and grace. You could also be dependent on family, friends, community and team members. I know I am every day.

We are social beings. We're not meant to do life alone. That's the power of interdependence. When you're aware of your contributions in line with interdependence, you appreciate the fact that your gifts, strengths and natural abilities are yours to use to help others; and their gifts, strengths and natural abilities are available to help you.

There's an African proverb that says, 'If you want to go fast, go alone; if you want to go far, go together.'[34] Yes, you can indeed go fast if you do things on your own, especially if you're the technician or subject matter expert. You don't have to consider others, communicate or collaborate, and you can get the job done effectively and efficiently on your own, but it's not a sustainable or scalable strategy. Be the leader who embraces cognitive diversity and thrives on the opportunity to teach, coach and raise others up, rather than doing things alone. Interdependence will accelerate your growth and amplify your impact.

If you want to increase your awareness of dependence and interdependence, ask yourself these questions:

- What is the situation I see?

- How do I value and appreciate others' contributions?

- Who is best suited to lead this project?

- Where do my strengths and limitations lie?

- How can I remove obstacles, including myself?

- Am I open to collaboration and input from others?

- How can we complement each other's skills?

- How do I nurture and maintain supportive relationships?

- What value do I bring to the table?

- Do I share knowledge and resources to help others grow?

- How do I manage conflicts for mutual benefit?

- Am I aware of the broader impact of my decisions and actions?

- How do I adapt to others' changing needs and expectations?

- Do I engage in networks that foster collaboration and support?

- How do I balance my personal needs with those of others?

The more you realise you don't need to do life or business alone, the quicker you'll look for opportunities to synergise and the faster you'll achieve your goals. By considering these questions, you will develop a greater awareness of your dependence on others and the importance of interdependence. This will enable you to build stronger relationships, collaborate more effectively and create mutually beneficial outcomes in your personal and professional lives.

Summary

As we conclude this chapter, it's crucial to remember that self-awareness, awareness of others, dependency and interdependency is an ongoing process and there's always room for growth. Embrace the journey of self-discovery and make a conscious effort to be intentional about your thoughts, words, actions and interactions with others. By cultivating awareness, you're laying the groundwork for personal mastery and professional excellence, empowering yourself to break through barriers and ultimately liberate your greatness. Keep reflecting, learning and growing, and watch as your new-found awareness transforms your life and career. All proactive change starts with awareness – that's the Principle of Awareness.

Practical application

Reflect on the Principle of Awareness

Reflection is a skill. Take a moment to capture your thoughts and commit to taking consistent action to move the needle forward.

- What key insights did you discover in this chapter?

- What decisions are you committed to making to gain the greatest return?

- What disciplined action will you take in the next week/month/quarter that will give you the greatest reward?

Activity

In the spirit of striving for excellence and continual improvement, what will you...

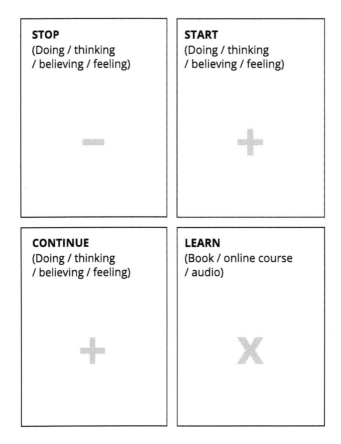

STOP
(Doing / thinking / believing / feeling)

START
(Doing / thinking / believing / feeling)

CONTINUE
(Doing / thinking / believing / feeling)

LEARN
(Book / online course / audio)

Additional resources

For bonus videos and downloadable content related to the Principle of Awareness, visit: www.liberateyourgreatness.com/awareness.

Explore our FiiT4GROWTH scorecards for greater self-awareness and team-awareness: www.fiit4growth.com/scorecards.

FOUR

The Principle Of Alignment

Alignment is key to liberating your greatness

The Principle of Alignment is a vital component of your path to greatness. Alignment is when you're living in congruence with the best of who you are and who you want to be and become. It's when you align your head and your heart. It ensures that every aspect of your life and career is working in harmony to achieve your goals.

The same applies when you're leading others. Having your team aligned on why they do what they do and how they're going to do it enables them to move forward in the right direction, together. In this chapter, we will delve into the process of aligning your purpose, people, mission, vision, values, goals, actions and habits to create a powerful synergy that propels you towards success, faster.

Alignment is a foundational key to happiness and the catalyst for unlocking your true potential. When you align your values with your actions, you can focus your energy, minimise distractions and make meaningful strides towards your dreams, goals and ambitions.

In the business realm, alignment brings hearts and minds together, uniting people with a common purpose. When your personal goals and values are in harmony with your organisation's mission and objectives, you'll naturally feel more motivated and engaged in your work. This leads to enhanced productivity and performance, ultimately benefiting the entire company.

Alignment also plays a crucial role in fostering effective communication and collaboration. It ignites the synergy necessary for success. When you and your team members are aligned, you can collaborate seamlessly, sharing a common vision and understanding of your company's goals. This creates a positive and productive work environment, resulting in improved teamwork and increased job satisfaction.

Why is alignment so critical in your efforts to liberate your greatness? It's because alignment ensures that your thoughts, words and actions are in sync with your purpose, people, mission, vision, values and goals. It may seem like a daunting task to align all these elements, but here's why it's essential...

Alignment is the compass that guides you towards your true north, keeping you on the path to greatness. When everything in your life is aligned, you'll be better equipped to overcome obstacles, seize opportunities and ultimately achieve the success and fulfilment you've always desired.

If you're misaligned, you'll feel miserable

If you are misaligned, you will be miserable. Consider your health, wealth and relationships:

- If you're unhappy about your mental, emotional, physical or spiritual well-being, it's because you're misaligned. Your thoughts, words and actions aren't aligned with the goals you're striving to achieve in those areas of your life. Perhaps your habits aren't setting you up to consistently succeed in areas of well-being.

- If you're feeling disengaged, disconnected and disillusioned at work, you're misaligned with the values, goals, objectives and behaviours of the organisation or its leadership. Potentially, there's no longer a good fit between you and them.

- If you're checked out of your friendships or significant relationship, it's because you're misaligned with each other's purpose, vision for the future, values and goals. Maybe you want different things from life.

- If your people are mentally and emotionally checked out, it's because they are misaligned with your vision and the direction you're going in. Even more detrimental to your business is when your people see that your actions are misaligned with your vision, values and purpose. The number of leaders I've seen publicly violating company values by verbally abusing their people in team meetings is astonishing. You can be kind and candid without being direct and destructive. Recognise that your intention and execution have an impact on others.

- If you don't have your values and principles aligned with your dream goals and daily activities, you will become SAD: stressed, anxious and depressed.

I've enjoyed great alignment in some of my business ventures and corporate roles and experienced the pain of misalignment, too. Trust me, alignment is better for everyone involved!

You're here for a reason

Why are you here? Why do you exist? Whenever I'm asked those questions, I instinctively answer:

> I exist to serve by liberating greatness for individuals, teams and businesses. It's why I'm here. It's what I do. I want to serve. I want to liberate greatness for DJAM (Daleen, my wife; Jewel, Anthony and Marcus, my precious children). I want to liberate greatness for you, for your team, for your business. I want to liberate greatness for my team and clients, family and friends, church and community.

That's taken me years of intentionality; deliberate choices on where I get involved and where I don't. I've walked away from business opportunities and clients, where I feel that the investment of my time, energy, resources, money and sanity are not worth the ROI for them and me. If it's an opportunity to liberate greatness, I'm in. If not, I'm out.

I'm on mission to connect, inspire, encourage and uplift everyone I serve, to improve their lives, accelerate their growth, achieve their goals faster and amplify their impact. I want to inspire hope for a better future.

I have a clear vision for my life, for my family, business, team and the world we want to contribute towards making better than it is today. From a business impact point of view, I see a world where individuals thrive personally and professionally; teams communicate, collaborate and co-create the future together; and businesses accelerate their growth and amplify their impact because they genuinely care for and support their people's MEPS Well-being® (mental, emotional, physical and spiritual well-being).

I strive to do that by bringing my values to life. I want to be enthusiastic, excellent and extraordinary:

- **Enthusiastic** – I always want to be full of genuine positivity, energy and joy in my interactions.

- **Excellent** – When you strive for excellence and do things with a spirit of excellence, success gravitates towards you.

- **Extraordinary** – Not because I want anyone to say I'm extraordinary, but because I want to be a person of *extra*! Extra energy, extra love, extra care, extra attention to detail, extra time, extra effort. I want people to know that I will go the extra mile for them so that I might inspire others to live, learn, love and grow every day.

My goals are aligned to who I need to become and what I need to do to see my vision become a reality, achieve my mission and fulfil my purpose. I must work on my actions and habits daily to maintain consistency and stay on track to creating an extraordinary life for my family, and helping my clients make an extraordinary impact in the world.

Your extraordinary life by design

Liberating your greatness is a pursuit; a journey to becoming extraordinary. Earlier in this book you defined what greatness means to you. I've been encouraging you from the beginning that greatness is within you. I also challenged you to recognise that while you have the potential for greatness, you must do the work required to earn and achieve that greatness in various aspects of your life. There will be a great ROI if you do – and there's a COI if you don't do the work.

How did all the greats of our time become extraordinary? They were ordinary people like you and I who chose to become extraordinary. In fact, they may have had tougher upbringings, more insecurities or an even harder struggle to navigate, yet somehow they managed to break through from survival to success and significance.

I had a personal trainer once called Baltz. He was short in stature, strong, fit and lean. Everything he taught me was about technique, mindset, and inner and physical strength. That made my workouts super-effective and efficient.

We used to train at 5:30am, and he would grill me through a combination of cardio and strength training. I remember texting him one morning saying that I wasn't feeling up for training and that I'd see him the following week. The message back from him was concise and crystal clear: 'Johno, get your ass out of bed, and get to the gym. I'm waiting for you.'

Off to the gym I went. I met Baltz and apologised for my attitude. After he politely lectured me about not wasting his time, my time and my money, he said something to me that has had a lasting impact in my life. He said, 'The only difference between ordinary and extraordinary is that little bit extra. If you want the results you've asked me to help you achieve, you must do more than everyone else around you.'

We all need a personal trainer or coach like Baltz – someone committed to calling us out on our own self-sabotage and challenging us to higher standards. You too can become extraordinary if you choose to commit to a life of being extraordinary and doing extraordinary things and then follow through with massive faith and courageous action.

Raise your standards if you want to become extraordinary. Be more. Do more. Have more. Be more extraordinary. Do more extraordinary things. Have more extraordinary experiences.

Set your sights to liberate your greatness

In the remainder of this chapter, I want to provide you with practical tools to gain greater clarity and purposeful direction with each of the elements on your own personal compass. Together, we'll explore the purpose, vision and values that will give you the focus you need to take the right action and build the right habits. We'll cover goals, action and habits in the next chapter.

Purpose: Discover your reason for being

Discovering why you do what you do is a gift to yourself and everyone around you. I've personally coached over 1,000 leaders, either one-to-one or in small groups, and have had the privilege of helping them define their purpose.

To start the process of self-discovery for my clients, one of the first things I have them do when we begin working together is to define three words that describe how they want to show up in the world and who they want to be as the most ideal version of themselves. They could be aspirational words or words that they would be proud to be described as, because these words describe the best of who they are or who they could be. This simple yet powerful exercise has been an absolute game-changer for me and my clients.

One of my dearest friends, client, mentor and fellow student-master Bill Noble has aligned his passion for 'seeing people grow' and his purpose of 'creating an environment for people to thrive' to guide his approach to acquiring and sharing knowledge. As a result, he consciously seeks out opportunities to understand and guide people on their journeys.[35]

My three words

Earlier in this chapter, as I was talking you through my purpose. I said, 'I want to be enthusiastic, excellent and extraordinary.' Those are my three words for how I want to show up for you and to everyone I serve.

Expanding on that principle, I have three words for how I want to show up in other areas of my life. When I'm writing, shooting videos or creating content, I want to be confident, courageous and creative. I use that to remind me to focus on my audience, serve them and deliver a message that has a positive, inspiring impact on them, personally and professionally.

For my children, I want to be present, kind and gentle. If I'm not mentally present (even though I may be physically present), I might not be kind or gentle. Instead, I'll be half-engaged, nodding at what they're saying but not giving them the undivided attention they need. I might even snap at them if I'm under pressure.

I don't know about you, but my kids can irritate me! When I'm on my phone or my laptop and my kids interrupt me, they irritate me. That feeling of irritation is a trigger for me, and it helps me realise that I'm the problem because I'm not present. The second I turn off distractions and get fully present, focused and engaged with my kids, that's when I see them for who they truly are; not irritating at all, but the most beautiful, unique, creative children that I'm blessed to have in my life.

Presence is one of the greatest gifts we can give to the people around us.

You can apply this three words exercise to so many different areas of your life, at home and at work. Designing how you interact with others and how you show up in the world, brings intentionality and deliberate action.

What are your three words?

What are your design principles for great relationships, excellence at work and a fulfilling life? How would people describe you? What are the words they would use to define your superpowers?

Here are a handful of examples from my clients to inspire you as you define yours:

- Thoughtful, engaging and Socratic

- Visionary, humble and enabling

- Energy, grace and love

- Loyal, fun and caring

- Present, disciplined and peaceful

- Confident, trustworthy, role model

- Fun, transformational and intuitive

- Confident, courageous and strong

- Caring, energetic and successful

Educate, empower, encourage

I've had the privilege of coaching Micah Johnson, former Major League Baseball player turned success-ful artist, NFT artist, creator and author of Aku, who also featured on the cover of *TIME* magazine. Micah is a wonderful human being, who's already achieved so much in his life. His purpose for Aku is to: 'Build worlds around dreams.'[36] I truly believe the best is yet to come from him and the impact he will have in the world. Helping Micah gain greater clarity on how he'll bring that purpose to life, he committed to being the best version of himself: confident, courageous, decisive and dependable. That's helped him make critical deci-sions for the future of the business.

Expanding the principle, all things Aku-related will now be deliberately designed to 'educate, empower and encourage'.[37] Those three words have brought laser-focused clarity to what Micah and the team cre-ate, and amplified the importance of why they do what they do. I can't wait to see what Micah creates next and the contribution he will add to the world.

Your purpose could save lives

In his book, *Man's Search for Meaning*,[38] Viktor E. Frankl describes his experiences as a Holocaust survivor and his observations of his fellow prisoners in Nazi con-centration camps. Frankl observed that those prisoners who were able to find a purpose or meaning in their lives – even under the direst circumstances – were more resilient and capable of enduring the tremendous suf-fering and hardship they faced. This sense of purpose gave them the strength to continue and to resist giving up, no matter how brutal their conditions. He acknowledged that his own sense of purpose helped him survive too. He observed, 'He who has a why to live, can bear with almost any how.'

There's a well-known parable of Christopher Wren and the construction of St. Paul's Cathedral.[39] Following the Great Fire of London in 1666, renowned architect Christopher Wren was called upon to design the new St. Paul's Cathedral. During the construction in 1971, Wren came across three bricklayers on a scaffold – one crouched, one half-standing and one standing tall – working diligently on the same wall. Curious about their perspectives, he asked each of them, 'What are you doing?'

The first bricklayer, focused on the task at hand, said, 'I'm a bricklayer, working hard to feed my family by laying bricks.'

The second bricklayer, with a broader perspective, replied, 'I'm a builder, constructing a wall for this magnificent structure.'

It was the third bricklayer who captured the essence of purpose, standing tall and beaming with pride, 'I'm a cathedral builder, creating a beautiful sanctuary to honour The Almighty.'

This parable of the three bricklayers has numerous interpretations, such as the importance of big-picture thinking, a positive attitude and connecting to an organisation's mission. Yet, at its core, the story is about purpose. The third bricklayer saw his work as a calling. He understood that each brick he laid contributed to something greater than himself. This sense of purpose transformed his attitude and gave profound meaning to his labour.

Leaders have a responsibility to encourage and support others in finding their purpose, or their 'cathedral'. As you liberate your greatness, ask yourself: How can I help others become cathedral builders, discovering their unique purpose in life? How can I guide them towards living out their calling with passion and excellence?

It's not just about the bricks you lay; it's about the cathedral you build. Serve ahead of the curve. Embrace your purpose and make a difference in the world around you.

Define your purpose

To find your purpose, start by asking yourself some important questions:

- What are you passionate about?

- What are your unique talents and abilities?

- What values and principles guide your life?

- How can you make a positive impact on the world?

Your answers to these questions will help you uncover your purpose and create a solid foundation for your personal and professional lives. This may evolve over time as you grow, learn and experience new things that clarify and solidify your purpose.

There are several brilliant frameworks to help you discover your purpose. One of my favourites is the ikigai framework, which originated from a Japanese concept that helps you discover your purpose by finding the intersection between four essential elements of life: passion, profession, vocation and mission. By exploring each of these elements, you can uncover your unique ikigai, or 'reason for being', which can bring a sense of fulfilment and happiness to your life.

Marc Winn, who describes himself as 'a way-finder, coffee shaman, mentor and adviser',[40] creatively connected various principles to create the ikigai framework, with a view to help people, organisations and communities find their ikigai and make their dreams come true. I've had coffee with Marc. He's a genuinely nice guy, with a heart to serve and make a positive impact in the world.

Here are the four essential elements of life in more detail.[41]

- **Passion** – What you love doing. Passion is about exploring your interests and hobbies, and the activities that bring you joy and excitement.

- **Profession** – What you are good at, or the skills and talents you have developed. Your profession is where your expertise and experience lie, allowing you to excel in your chosen field.

- **Vocation** – What the world needs, or how you can contribute to society. Your vocation is about identifying the problems and challenges that you feel called to address, making a positive impact on others and the world around you.

- **Mission** – What you can be paid for, or the ways you can earn a living by leveraging your skills and passions. Your mission is about finding opportunities to turn your passion and expertise into a sustainable income.

By reflecting on each of these elements and finding the common ground between them, you can discover your unique ikigai. This self-awareness helps you to align your life choices with your purpose, leading to a more fulfilling, purpose-driven life. Embracing your ikigai can also help you stay motivated, focused and resilient, as you have a clear understanding of why you are doing what you do and the impact you want to create.

Align your life choices with your purpose

I've gone into real depth on purpose, because having clarity of your purpose is like having a North Star guiding your thoughts, words and actions. When you align your life choices with your purpose – when you live a purpose-driven life – you will make a positive, significant impact on the world and in the lives of those around you. Let's explore the other areas that are critical to alignment in your personal and professional lives. You have a choice in all of these:

- **People** – Surrounding yourself with the right people can make all the difference in your pursuit of a purpose-driven life. When you align yourself with individuals who share your values, support your goals and contribute positively to your growth, you'll find that your journey towards greatness becomes more enjoyable and fulfilling.

- **Mission** – Your mission outlines what you strive to achieve and the impact you want to make. When your actions align with your mission, you'll find the path to success becomes clearer.

- **Vision** – A compelling vision paints a vivid picture of the future you desire. Aligning your actions with your vision ensures you're always moving towards the realisation of that future.

- **Values** – Your values are the core beliefs that guide your behaviour and decision-making. When you align your actions with your values, you'll experience greater integrity and authenticity in everything you do.

- **Goals** – Clear, specific goals provide milestones on your journey to greatness. Aligning your actions with your goals allows you to measure progress and stay on track, ensuring you're always moving forward.

- **Actions** – Purposeful actions are the steps you take to turn your aspirations into reality. Aligning your actions with your purpose, mission, vision, values and goals ensures that every step you take is propelling you towards the life you desire and the impact you want to make.

- **Habits** – Consistent, purposeful actions lead to consistent, purposeful habits, which are the building blocks of success. Aligning your habits with your purpose, mission, vision, values and goals helps to create a powerful, focused daily routine that accelerates your journey towards liberation.

We'll explore people, goals, actions and habits in the upcoming chapters. For the remainder of this chapter on alignment, let's dive into vision and values.

Vision: What do you see?

In the pursuit of greatness, having a clear vision is just as important as knowing your purpose. Proverbs 29:18 says, 'Where there is no vision, the people perish.'[42] Your vision is the destination you're striving for, the vivid mental image of what you want to achieve and where you want to be in the future. The people you lead are counting on you to clearly articulate your vision. By defining your vision, you create a roadmap that guides your actions and helps you stay on course towards achieving your dreams.

In my coffee shop days, there was an art gallery across the passage from my store, owned by a well-known and well-liked South African painter, Joe Marais. Joe's work has been seen in solo exhibitions in Canada, Mauritius and the US. Drawing inspiration from wild-life, landscapes and cityscapes, his acrylic-on-canvas works are photographic in their realism, capturing not only the exact colours and textures of his subjects, but also distilling movement and emotion onto canvas.[43]

Whenever I would notice Joe putting a blank canvas on his easel to begin creating a new masterpiece, I would go up to him and ask, 'Joe, what do you see?' He would smile, look at the blank canvas for a brief moment and then start describing to me in rich detail the landscape, animals and mood he envisioned. He'd talk about the way the sunlight would cast its warm, golden rays on the scene, how the majestic animals would move gracefully through their environment, and the sense of awe and wonder he hoped to evoke through his brushstrokes.

Over the course of several days or even weeks, I'd watch as Joe meticulously brought his vision to life, stroke by stroke, layer by layer. Each time I passed by his gallery, I would smile and marvel at the transformation taking place on the canvas, secretly knowing that I had the privilege of a 'first glimpse' before he put brush to canvas. From seemingly random brushstrokes and patches of colour, an incredible work of art would emerge, embodying the essence of the scene he had described to me earlier.

One day, as I watched Joe putting the final touches on a breathtaking painting of a lion pride in the African grasslands, I realised that there was a powerful lesson to be learnt from his creative process. Just like Joe, we all have our own blank canvases in life. What a gift when we're able to appreciate the blank canvas in front of us, envision our future, our goals and dreams, and then take the necessary steps, stroke by stroke, to bring them to life. That requires clarity, patience, persistence and unwavering belief in our own vision, even when others may not yet see the masterpiece taking shape.

Joe's artistic journey is a beautiful reminder that our lives are works in progress. With dedication and focus, we can transform our blank canvases into masterpieces that not only capture our unique passions and experiences but also inspire others to embrace their own journeys of self-discovery and growth.

Nikos Kazantzakis, a famous Greek writer and philosopher, once said, 'You have your brush, you have your colours, you paint the paradise, then in you go.'[44] I love the uninhibited simplicity of Nikos' guidance. He beautifully encapsulates the idea that we are the artists of our own lives with the power to shape our reality through our thoughts, actions and attitudes. By embracing our creative potential and taking ownership of our personal growth, we can paint our own unique vision of paradise and then step into the masterpiece we've created.

As you embark on your journey of self-discovery and personal mastery, remember that you hold the brush and the colours to create the life you truly desire. Let your imagination guide you, and never be afraid to boldly paint your dreams into existence.

Clarity brings colour, peace, power and focus

As a leader, it's as important for you to have a clear vision for your life and future as it is to have a clear vision for your team and business. What bold ambition would you like to achieve? How will you and your team like to make a positive, significant impact in the lives of your colleagues, customers and end users? When you're sharing a vision, let people borrow your eyes so that they can see what you see.

I was coaching two incredible women recently, the CEO and COO of a businesswomen's club and network, who both have such a passion for diversity, equity, inclusion and belonging, with a specific drive to close the gender pay gap. They were preparing for an exclusive, by-invitation-only networking event in New York City. They wanted to fine-tune their messaging themes so that they could show up with clarity, confidence and courage, make a positive impression, build their network, secure funds for future development of their programmes and bring people on the journey with them.

Together, we finessed the vision and drive that was already inside both of them but wasn't yet clear or particularly inspiring. We first spent two hours understanding their audience, who they're serving and what they wanted to achieve at the event, to gain greater clarity and focus. Over the following week, I then had them create a pitch, which we reviewed in a one-hour 'pitch and polish' session a week later. What a powerful session! As they pitched, I challenged them to make their messaging clearer, more concise, more inspiring, more challenging.

Clarity brings colour. Clarity brings peace. Clarity brings power. Clarity brings focus. I remember getting goosebumps listening to them pitch the final version of their vision. Now I too can see the world they want to create, in rich colour, with absolute certainty that it will be a better world for all. That's the power of having a clear vision.

Creating your vision: Where are you going?

To create your own personal vision, begin by imagining your ideal future. Consider the following questions:

- What do you want to achieve in your personal and professional lives?
- What kind of person do you want to be?

- How do you want to be remembered?

- What legacy do you want to leave behind?

Now get emotionally connected to your vision by envisioning your future. Answer these questions:

- What would your best future self be experiencing in five years' time? In ten years?

- What would your best future self thank you for thinking, believing, feeling and doing between now and then?

- What would your best future self encourage you to think, believe, feel and do today?

Take time to reflect on these questions and visualise the life you want to create. Once you have a clear picture in your mind, write it down to solidify your commitment to your vision. I'd encourage you to complete this exercise with your team, too. People buy in to what they create, so co-create the vision with them. That way you'll be able to say that it's *our* vision, not just your vision.

As a leader, give your people formal permission to explore their potential and guide them towards their next level of growth and achievement – a VISA:

- **Vision** – Provide a clear, compelling vision for the future that aligns with their personal and professional goals. Help them understand how their role contributes to the bigger picture and encourage them to visualise their desired outcomes. By connecting to a meaningful vision, your people will feel more motivated and invested in their work, driving them to excel.

- **Inspiration** – Foster a culture of inspiration by celebrating successes, sharing motivational stories and leading by example. Encourage creativity, innovation and continuous learning, and provide opportunities for your people to grow and develop new skills. By inspiring them to push their boundaries, they will be more likely to reach their full potential.

- **Situation** – Cultivate situational awareness by understanding the unique strengths, weaknesses, opportunities and challenges your people face. Create an environment that encourages open communication and feedback, allowing your people to share their perspectives and insights. By being attuned to the current situation, you can make informed decisions and provide the support and resources needed for your people to thrive.

- **Access** – Grant your people access to the tools, resources and opportunities they need to succeed. This includes providing training and development programmes, mentorship and networking opportunities, as well as fostering a supportive work environment where collaboration and innovation can flourish. By offering access to valuable resources, you empower your people to grow, learn and excel in their roles.

Values: How you do something is how you do everything

At the heart of everything you do, think, say and achieve are your values. These principles serve as your personal guide, shaping your behaviour and decision-making processes. They provide a framework for how you navigate life, interact with others and pursue your goals. By understanding and embracing your values, you can create a strong foundation for your journey towards greatness and maintain a consistent alignment with your purpose, mission, vision and goals.

The world's highest performers are remarkably clear on what they value most in life. What do *you* value most in life? How do you define happiness and success?

Steven Bartlett, creator and host of the podcast *The Diary of a CEO with Steven Bartlett*, started a tradition for each guest to write down a question that he would then ask the next guest on his show. Bear Grylls OBE's question for the next guest to answer was: 'What is the greatest wealth in your life?'[45] What a powerful question to ask! The answer is bound to reveal someone's true values.

Matthew 6:21 states: 'For where your treasure is, there your heart will be also.'[46] Your priorities, values and affections are connected to what you consider important or valuable in life. If your 'treasure' lies in material wealth, your heart and focus will be on accumulating possessions. If your treasure lies in relationships, helping others, making a positive impact and living a meaningful life, your heart will be focused on those aspects. This is such a great reminder to consider where we place our value and attention as it reveals the true state of our heart and the priorities that guide our lives.

The power of having clear values

A good friend of mine and founder of Daddy Saturday,[47] Justin Batt, refers to the faithful five areas of his life, wherein he always wants to be intentional and impactful:

1. Faith

2. Family

3. Fitness

4. Friends

5. Finances

He brings those elements to life for himself, his family and everyone he teaches and encourages through his work. Daddy Saturday is a platform to equip dads with the tools to create epic experiences with their kids and empower fatherless kids through education and mentorship, giving them the foundation to own their future and experience the love of a father.

Bushido by Inazō Nitobe mentions the eight virtues of a Samurai being:[48]

1. Morality

2. Courage

3. Compassion

4. Politeness

5. Honesty and sincerity

6. Respect

7. Loyalty

8. Character and self-control

These eight virtues can have profound relevance in leadership and personal development, which is a key theme in *Liberate Your Greatness*. Each virtue is a powerful quality that, when embraced and practised, can contribute to one's journey towards greatness. Just as a Samurai hones these virtues to become a master warrior, leaders can adopt and refine these qualities to unlock their full potential, leading with greater clarity, confidence and compassion. These virtues not only contribute to personal mastery but also resonate with the principles of professional excellence, fostering a healthier, more productive environment in any organisation.

The virtues of greatness

In addition to the virtues listed above, the ten virtues of greatness are qualities or traits that are commonly associated with individuals who have achieved significant success or made a positive impact in their personal or professional lives:

1. **Service** – Great individuals often have a strong desire to help others and make a positive difference in the world. They value contribution and selflessness.

2. **Resilience** – The ability to bounce back from setbacks and adversity, and to keep going even when faced with challenges.

3. **Perseverance** – The determination and persistence to work towards a goal or vision, despite obstacles and setbacks.

4. **Courage** – The willingness to take risks, confront fears and face challenges with confidence.

5. **Integrity** – The adherence to a set of moral or ethical principles, honesty and transparency.

6. **Humility** – The ability to recognise and acknowledge one's own limitations and weaknesses, and to seek help or advice when needed.

7. **Empathy** – The ability to understand and share the feelings of others, and to act with compassion and kindness towards them.

8. **Creativity** – The ability to think outside the box and come up with innovative solutions to problems.

9. **Discipline** – The ability to control impulses, stay focused and follow through on commitments.

10. **Passion** – The intense enthusiasm and commitment towards a particular goal or activity.

These virtues can help you overcome obstacles, achieve success and make a positive impact in your personal and professional lives. With my passion for mastery and the martial arts, you can appreciate how I might resonate with these virtues. Which ones speak to you?

In many ways, your values become the design principles for how you do life – and hence how you do everything. Your values have the power to transform your life and the lives of all those around you. Every great brand has clear design principles; every great person has resolute values or design principles they bring to life daily.

17 design principles that guide my life

You will all have your own values to guide your life. It's well worth writing them down, reminding yourself of them often and doing your best to bring them to life. Below, I list the seventeen principles that guide my life:

1. My attitude determines my attitude.

2. Actions speak louder than words.

3. Work smarter and harder.

4. Stay hungry, stay humble.

5. Take responsibility for your past, present and future.

6. Private victories precede public victories.

7. Enthusiasm is positively infectious.

8. Excellence is the gradual result of always striving to be better.

9. The only difference between ordinary and extraordinary is that little bit extra.

10. Mastery takes time. Transformation takes time.

11. Go hard on the plan and easy on yourself.

12. Be present, kind and gentle.

13. Be bold, be brave, be brilliant.

14. Iron sharpens iron.

15. When the people serve win, I win.

16. Live, learn, love and grow every day.

17. Do everything with faith, hope and love.

Summary

On your quest to liberate your greatness, I want you to define and fulfil your purpose and positively impact the people you're called to serve through your mission, vision and values. In the next chapter, we'll look at the goals, actions and habits that bring it all to life.

Remember that achieving true alignment is an ongoing endeavour that requires dedication, reflection and adaptability. Continuously evaluate your sense of alignment to ensure all the elements remain in harmony and support your aspirations. Embrace the power of alignment to unlock your full potential and watch as it fuels your journey towards greatness.

Keep striving for alignment in all areas of your life, and you'll soon experience the profound impact it can have on your personal and professional success and the world around you. Aligning purpose, people, mission, vision, values and goals leads to laser-focused actions and habits – that's the Principle of Alignment.

Practical application

Reflect on the Principle of Alignment

Reflection is a skill. Take a moment to capture your thoughts and commit to taking consistent action to move the needle forward:

- What key insights did you discover in this chapter?

- What decisions are you committed to making to gain the greatest return?

- What disciplined action will you take in the next week/month/quarter that will give you the greatest reward?

Activity

In the spirit of striving for excellence and continual improvement, what will you...

STOP
(Doing / thinking / believing / feeling)

START
(Doing / thinking / believing / feeling)

CONTINUE
(Doing / thinking / believing / feeling)

PERSONAL DEVELOPMENT THIS MONTH
(Book / online course / audio)

X

Additional resources

For bonus videos and downloadable content related to the Principle of Alignment, visit www.liberateyourgreatness.com/alignment.

PART THREE

IMPLEMENTATION

In a world where it is so readily available, often information is not your problem; implementation is. You know what you need to do, but how can you do it effectively and efficiently?

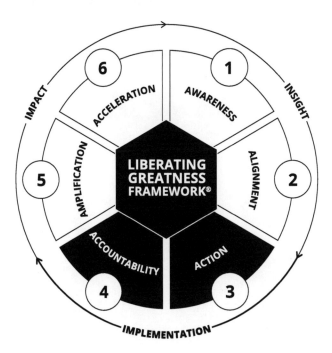

This part of *Liberate Your Greatness* is all about taking action and embracing accountability. With a solid foundation of awareness and alignment, you'll be prepared to implement strategies and make deliberate choices that drive you towards your goals. This section will provide you with the tools, techniques and motivation to transform your insights into tangible results, helping you to build momentum and create lasting change in your life.

As you work through Part Three, remember that the key to achieving greatness lies in your ability to take consistent, focused action. Accountability to yourself and others ensures you stick to the plan. By applying the principles and strategies presented here, you'll develop the discipline and determination required to overcome obstacles, stay committed to your goals and build unstoppable momentum.

FIVE

The Principle Of Action

Your answer is always in your activity

The Principle of Action is the driving force behind your quest for greatness, as it transforms your aspirations and plans into tangible results. You must take action! You cannot achieve success without it.

In this chapter, we will explore the importance of taking consistent, purposeful action in the pursuit of your goals, and how this approach can help you overcome obstacles and achieve your goals faster. We will also discuss various strategies and techniques for increasing productivity and maximising your effectiveness and efficiency, ensuring that you stay focused and committed to achieving your dreams.

With great awareness and alignment, your action will be laser-focused. Without it, your action will be scattered, haphazard and inconsistent – and at best will just keep you busy without achieving anything.

As Joel Barker said, 'Vision without action is merely a dream. Action without vision just passes time. Vision with action can change the world.'[49]

Living a purpose-driven life

Now that you've identified your purpose and aligned it with your mission, vision and values, embrace it wholeheartedly and make it the driving force behind your actions.

Actions to take to live a purpose-driven life

1. **Break your vision into meaningful, manageable goals** – Divide your vision into smaller, achievable milestones. This will make it easier to track your progress and maintain your motivation. Align your goals with your purpose to ensure that every step you take is leading you closer to your true potential.

2. **Develop an action plan** – Create a detailed plan outlining the steps you need to take to bring your vision to fruition. This will help you stay focused and ensure that your actions are aligned with your ultimate goals.

3. **Surround yourself with like-minded people** – Build a supportive network of individuals who share your values and aspirations. Together, you'll be able to encourage and inspire each other.

4. **Monitor your results, learn and grow** – To fulfil your purpose, you must always be willing to

improve and evolve. Embrace new challenges and experiences that stretch your limits and help you become the best version of yourself.

5. **Prioritise self-care** – Nurturing your MEPS Well-being is crucial to living a purpose-driven life. Make time for activities that nourish your soul and help you maintain balance.

6. **Celebrate your achievements** – Acknowledge and celebrate every success along the way, no matter how small. This will keep your motivation high and remind you of the progress you're making towards your vision.

7. **Give back** – Use your time, talents and treasure to make a positive impact on the lives of others. Contributing to the greater good not only deepens your sense of purpose but also enriches the lives of those around you.

Remember, your purpose is the essence of who you are and the driving force behind your actions. When you live with intention and make decisions based on your purpose, you can truly unlock your greatness to create a fulfilling, meaningful life.

From goals to greatness

To liberate your greatness, it's essential to have goals. You need a target to hit; something to aim for; something to work towards achieving. Goals provide direction, focus and motivation, guiding you on your path to greatness.

The SMART framework

The SMART framework[50] is a widely used approach to goal setting that encourages the creation of clear, specific and achievable objectives. The framework was first introduced in the early 1980s by George T. Doran, a consultant and former director of corporate planning for the Washington Water Power company, in a paper titled 'There's a S.M.A.R.T. Way to Write Management's Goals and Objectives'. The acronym stands for: specific, measurable, achievable (or attainable), realistic (or relevant) and time-bound.

The SMART framework provides a structure to help individuals and organisations set goals that are both challenging and attainable. While I like SMART, I don't love it. Although the framework has its merits, see if you can pick up which elements I'd change.

A brief overview of SMART components

- **S = Specific** – Your goal should be specific (well-defined and unambiguous), making it clear what needs to be achieved. This aspect of the framework addresses the 'who', 'what', 'where', 'when' and 'why' of the goal.

- **M = Measurable** – When your goal is quantifiable, you can track progress and determine when you've achieved it. Establishing measurable criteria ensures that you can monitor your progress and stay motivated.

- **A = Achievable (or attainable)** – An achievable goal is realistic, considering the resources, constraints and other factors that might impact your ability to accomplish the objective. This aspect of the framework encourages you to set challenging but attainable goals, which helps to maintain motivation and may prevent feelings of frustration or disappointment.

- **R = Realistic (or relevant)** – A realistic or relevant goal is aligned with broader objectives, priorities and values. This component ensures that the goal is worthwhile and contributes meaningfully to your or your organisation's overall vision.

- **T = Time-bound** – A time-bound goal has a specific deadline or timeframe for completion. This aspect of the framework creates a sense of urgency and encourages you to focus on your goals and prioritise your time effectively.

By using the SMART goals framework, you can create well-defined objectives that are likely to be achieved and may leave you feeling satisfied and successful. To me, though, SMART feels too safe. It's comfortable, doable, but a little underwhelming. You should know by now that I want you to get uncomfortable and out of your comfort zone because that's where the magic happens! Who's to say what's achievable and realistic? Why limit our thinking to predetermined levels of what's possible?

The great Nelson Mandela, also known affectionately to South Africans as 'Madiba' (the highly respected and endeared elder of the clan), said in numerous speeches, 'It always seems impossible until it's done.'[51] He knew that he needed to elevate his perception of possibility to become president of South Africa after twenty-seven years in prison. He knew he would have to lead and persuade a divided nation of 40 million South Africans bound for civil war to unity, peace and reconciliation. The Nelson Mandela era is arguably the greatest part of South Africa's history to date. Imagine if he'd only set a SMART goal!

I want you to set challenging, inspiring, uplifting goals. Goals that scare and excite you at the same time. Goals that will certainly leave you frustrated and disappointed in the beginning because they're difficult to achieve. Goals that will force you to level up your mindset, skillset and toolset to have any hope of ever achieving them. Goals you can't achieve on your own.

If I asked you to grow your sales by 10% in the next twelve months, that would be a SMART incremental goal – and you've had some solid strategies to achieve that. If I challenged you, on the other hand, to multiply your business by ten in the next twelve months, that would be an exponential goal, requiring you to think and behave differently to achieve it.

Introducing DREAM Goals™

While the SMART goals framework is useful for creating realistic and achievable objectives, it may not always be enough to inspire extraordinary growth and innovation. To truly achieve greatness it's essential to aim higher and strive for goals that are not only realistic but also truly inspiring. That's where DREAM Goals – a framework to inspire and encourage exponential growth – comes into play.

I designed the DREAM Goals framework to spark new levels of thinking, attitudes and behaviours that lead to exponential growth and success.

DARING   RESOLUTE   EXPANSIVE   ADAPTIVE   MOTIVATING

The components of DREAM Goals

- **D = Daring** – DREAM Goals should be bold and audacious, pushing you beyond your comfort zone and encouraging you to think big. Daring goals will challenge your assumptions, inspire innovation and drive you to explore new possibilities.

- **R = Resolute** – DREAM Goals require unwavering commitment and determination. A resolute goal means having clarity and conviction, a firm decision to pursue it relentlessly and an unwavering belief in your ability to achieve it, despite challenges or setbacks. It aligns with your purpose, vision, mission and values, and therefore raises your necessity to achieve it.

- **E = Expansive** – DREAM Goals should lead to significant growth, whether in terms of personal development, professional success or impact on the world around you. An expansive goal will encourage you to expand your horizons, broaden your perspectives and continuously evolve.

- **A = Adaptive** – DREAM Goals should encourage testing, failing, learning and improving. Adaptive goals are flexible and dynamic, allowing you to monitor and measure your results and adjust your approach based on changing circumstances, new insights or emerging opportunities. This adaptability ensures that you can continue to strive for your goal, even when faced with unexpected challenges.

- **M – Motivating** – DREAM Goals should be deeply motivating and energising, driving you to take action and persevere, even when the going gets tough. Motivating goals will provide a clear sense of purpose and direction, keeping you focused and excited about the journey ahead, while also inspiring those around you to join you on your mission.

The DREAM Goals framework challenges you to think beyond conventional goal setting to strive for greatness. By embracing daring, resolute, expansive, adaptive and motivating goals, you can unlock exponential growth and unleash your true potential. With DREAM Goals firmly in place, it's time for taking massive action!

To access the DREAM Goals templates, go to www.liberateyourgreatness/dreamgoals.

Guiding principles for taking massive action

As an entrepreneur or business leader, you must understand that the results you achieve are directly linked to the actions you take. If you have great ambition, you must take massive action. Your answer is always in your activity. By evaluating the effectiveness of your daily actions, you can pinpoint areas for improvement and adjust your efforts accordingly.

Your action must reflect your ambition

Action is the key that turns your thoughts, intentions and ambitions into tangible achievements. It's a vital component of both personal and professional growth, as it empowers you to transform your dreams and aspirations into reality. As Albert Einstein said, 'Nothing happens until something moves.'[52]

Actions speak louder than words. It's important to have great ambitions if you want to make a significant impact in your work. Think it, speak it and then take massive action to bring it to life. To ensure you're focusing on the right activities, create a list of high-leverage tasks that contribute to your long-term goals. Prioritise these tasks and develop a plan to consistently work on them. As you do, measure your progress and adjust your approach as needed. By doing so, you'll maintain momentum and make significant strides towards liberating your greatness.

My dad always used to encourage me to work smarter, not harder. I appreciate the fact that he didn't necessarily want me working the long hours he did in his retail stores, and that he valued the power of knowledge and skills to accelerate growth. Throughout my corporate, consulting, coaching and entrepreneurial experiences, I've come to value a combination of working smarter and harder.

Dwayne 'The Rock' Johnson challenges his audience to 'Be the hardest worker in the room.'[53] That's a strategy that's worked out well for him. As a result of his incredible work ethic, focus and talent – and of course, his ability to raise his right eyebrow and smoulder – he's a role model when it comes to working smarter and harder.

In my honours year at the University of Cape Town, amid attending lectures and writing my thesis, I waited on tables at a sports café twice a week, tutored third year marketing students and worked at the reception of a local gym, the Health & Racquet Club, once a week (partly for the free gym membership, partly for the extra cash and partly for the free lunch at the taster stations of a nearby premium supermarket). I also sold nutrition products through a direct sales company and I sang in a two-piece band, Maroon City, with one of my best friends, Toby, once a week for ladies' night at a local pub. Picture it… two young lads, two guitars, two voices in perfect rhythm and harmony in a jam-packed pub – it always made for a fantastic Wednesday night! At the end of the year, I was the one in my marketing honours class that got offered jobs by all three companies I applied to: Ogilvy & Mather, Procter & Gamble and Unilever. They could see the focus, drive and energy I had to take action and make things happen! I didn't get top marks for my thesis, but I loved writing it and gained so much more in the process.

Early in my consulting career, I had a mentor, Derek Botha, who showed me the benefits of 'walking the leather, doing the hard yards, getting your shoes dirty!' He recognised the simple, highly effective skill of spending time with clients, walking the corridors with them, understanding their needs and being present for opportunities to support them because he was immersed in their business.

Following in his footsteps, so to speak, I too 'walked the leather', spending quality time with my corporate clients, understanding their needs and making myself available to help them solve major problems. One of those clients was a large international food manufacturer who wanted to build their sales team capability. In previous years, they spent in the region of £40,000 per year on ad hoc training with the consultancy.

While that did have some impact on the team's capability, it didn't result in significantly positive change. So, I spent six months understanding their needs and working closely with them to design something fresh and relevant. I then created a sales academy for them, which would have everyone in their sales organisation – from sales reps all the way through to their sales directors – go through a three-year programme consisting of quarterly learning courses, assignments and assessments.

The entire academy was mapped to tertiary education unit standards and accredited. At the end of the three years, learners would receive a diploma in sales at various levels. The company invested £1.8 million in the sales academy over a period of five years (forty-five times their previous average annual investment). In return, they received a game-changing solution to their sales capability that far exceeded their investment. In addition to building their sales capability, the sales academy became a recruitment and retention tool for the best talent in their industry. They had great ambition and took massive action.

Consider the ROI and COI

Talk is cheap, action pays the bills. You must act. As Wayne Gretzky says, 'You miss 100% of the shots you don't take.'[54] Far too often, teams have inspiring conversations but leave meetings without clarity on what they're supposed to do next and therefore they don't do anything or take incohesive action.

Whenever I facilitate strategy sessions or leadership workshops for senior leadership teams, I challenge participants to have great conversations that lead to commitments, action plans and accountability. That sets the tone for the duration of the workshop, where every topic covered requires conversation, discussion and input from everyone present, and then we capture commitments, action plans and accountability measures.

Transitioning from conversation to commitment and action requires decisions and allocating resources. It's important to consider both the potential ROI and the COI. ROI allows you to assess the financial impact of your choices, ensuring that you're investing time and money into activities that will yield the greatest results. On the other hand, COI forces you to consider the consequences of *not* taking action. What if you don't do anything? What's the cost to you? This can be a powerful motivator, as it highlights the potential losses and missed opportunities that may result from inaction. By considering both the ROI and COI, you can make more informed decisions and take calculated risks to propel your business forward.

One of my celebrity entrepreneur clients initially approached me because she was losing $250,000 per month in her business and needed some guidance, clarity and support. Having achieved early success in her online business, she had built up a team of heavyweights set to take the business to new heights. Unfortunately, her block-chain-based industry was disrupted, which negatively impacted her business model. Her confidence was at an all-time low and she felt she lacked the courage to make tough decisions. Understanding her purpose, mission, vision and values enabled me to see a path forward for her. She clearly wasn't getting an ROI, and there was a significant COI. If she didn't change soon, she would lose everything.

Within a few weeks of working with her, we restructured the team, created a new vision and established core values and three DREAM Goals, refocusing the team on revenue-generating opportunities. We generated almost $2 million per year in savings and opened new revenue streams to create a sustainable, profitable business. I'm proud of her for having the humility to seek support and openness to pivot in a new direction for a better future for herself and the business. I'm excited to see what she creates for the world.

Decision empowers you; indecision disempowers you

I learnt this lesson from André Olivier, senior pastor at Rivers Church in South Africa, where I had the privilege of serving in the worship team for several years. Deciding – even if it's not the perfect decision – empowers you to take control of your life and business.

Darren Hardy, another of my mentors and success coaches, emphasises the idea that success begins with a decision and requires subsequent action. That's how you succeed: one empowering decision followed by action, followed by more empowering decisions and actions.

Decision allows you to move forward, learn, adapt and grow. It propels you towards your goals and helps you build momentum. Indecision, on the other hand, leaves you stagnant and vulnerable to external forces, often leading to feelings of helplessness. 'Indecision is the thief of opportunity', as Jim Rohn often described it.[55]

Every day we have decisions to make at home and at work. Choices on what we think, feel, do and therefore experience in life. Even when things aren't going our way, we can choose how to respond to the situation.

When I have moments of self-doubt or a negative narrative swirling around in my head, I remind myself that life is all about choices.

Choices I create to help me stay focused and inspired

- **Choose faith over fear** – Faith and fear are both rooted in belief. While faith is the belief in something positive and empowering, fear is the belief in potential negative outcomes. As an entrepreneur or business leader, it's crucial to choose faith over fear to unlock your true potential and liberate your greatness. Choose to look up, look in and look forward.

  As stated in Hebrews 11:1, 'Now faith is confidence in what we hope for and assurance about what we do not see.'[56] Trust God, believe in yourself and trust the journey, even when the outcome is uncertain. Have confidence in your ability to overcome challenges and achieve your goals.

- **Choose courage over comfort** – Courage is not the absence of fear but rather the ability to act in spite of it. You must be willing to step out of your comfort zone and confront challenges head-on. Magic happens outside of your comfort zone. It's through facing your fears and taking risks that you experience the most growth. By demonstrating courage, you'll cultivate resilience and unlock your true potential.

- **Choose change over stagnation** – Change leads to growth. It's a fundamental law of nature: you're either growing or you're dying. Embrace the inevitability of change and be open to new experiences and perspectives. Strive to consistently expand your knowledge, skills and perspectives, so you can continue to develop both personally and professionally.

- **Choose self-improvement over self-sabotage** – Seek to enhance your self-awareness, address your weaknesses and build on your strengths, instead of undermining your own success through negative self-talk or self-destructive behaviours. By choosing self-improvement, you demonstrate a commitment to becoming the best version of yourself.

- **Choose progress over perfection** – If you wait until the conditions are perfect, you'll never take any meaningful action. Striving for perfection leads to procrastination. Don't wait for perfect timing or perfect circumstances; take imperfect action. Prioritise making incremental improvements and celebrating small wins instead of striving for an unattainable ideal of perfection. Recognise that mistakes and setbacks are part of the journey and use them as setups for your next level and opportunities to learn and grow. By choosing progress, you build momentum and resilience, propelling you closer to your goals.

- **Choose experience over complacency** – Seek out opportunities to learn, grow and expand your horizons. Value the wisdom gained from experiences, both good and bad, as they shape who you are and who you will become. These will guide your future thinking and behaviour and equip you with hindsight to guide others.

- **Choose adventure over familiarity** – Dare to explore new paths, meet new people and try new things. Embrace the excitement of the unknown and let it fuel your passion for life. Adventure builds courage and resilience and helps you discover your true potential. By choosing adventure, you'll live a more vibrant, fulfilling life and create memories that will last a lifetime.

- **Choose gratitude over entitlement** – Cultivate a sense of thankfulness and appreciation for what you have, rather than focusing on what you believe you're owed. Gratitude fosters a positive mindset, improves relationships and increases overall happiness. By choosing gratitude, you acknowledge the many blessings already in your life and open yourself to more opportunities and experiences.

- **Choose collaboration over competition** – Embrace the power of teamwork and cooperation, recognising that by working together you can achieve more than you could alone. Foster a culture of mutual support and shared goals, rather than pitting yourself against others in a zero-sum game. By choosing collaboration, you create an environment where everyone can thrive and contribute to collective success.

- **Choose contribution over consumption** – Focus on giving back and making a positive impact on the world, rather than solely seeking personal gain or material possessions. Strive to leave a legacy and contribute to the greater good through acts of kindness, mentorship or community involvement. By choosing contribution, you enrich your life and the lives of others, while also fostering a sense of purpose and fulfilment, and you do so without judgement.

Which of the above resonate with you? Incorporate any of these choices into your own life or use them as inspiration to create your own list. The key is to focus on empowering and positive choices that can help shape a fulfilling, successful life. You always have options, choices and decisions to make.

Tony Robbins has often emphasised the importance of decision-making, famously asserting, 'It's in the moment of decision that your destiny is shaped.'[57] In that instant when you decide, you set your sights on a new destination. Many people make the mistake of deciding, making a bold commitment and then falling short of taking the action required to follow through and achieve the results they desire. Decision alone is not enough – you must take action.

By making decisions and committing to a course of action, you cultivate a sense of self-confidence and self-efficacy. Embrace the fact that not every decision will be perfect but understand that indecision can be far more costly than making a mistake. So, take charge of your life, make decisions with conviction and watch as your power to create, innovate and achieve your goals is unleashed.

Start before you're ready

A common pitfall for entrepreneurs and business leaders is the tendency to wait for the 'perfect' moment to take action. The truth is, there will never be a perfect time to start. Instead, you must embrace the mindset of starting before you're ready. This means taking action despite uncertainty and using the learning process to refine your approach.

In his compelling wisdom, Steven Furtick once said, 'The success rate on seeds that are not sown: zero percent. There is a hundred percent mortality of unsown seeds.'[58] This profound truth urges us to take action, understanding that our efforts are the prerequisite for any potential growth and success.

Action comes from having clarity on what you need to do and then having the courage to stand up, step out and figure things out along the way. Accept and embrace the fact that much of your growth will happen between the start and the finish line. You must start to experience that growth.

When you adopt this mentality, you'll find that your progress accelerates as you gain valuable experience and insights. As you face challenges and overcome obstacles, you'll develop resilience and confidence in your ability to achieve your goals. Action leads to newfound awareness, and awareness is the foundation for liberating your greatness. So, don't wait for the perfect moment; seize the opportunity and start now.

Nike, one of the world's most recognised sports brands, has a slogan that has become synonymous with taking action: 'Just Do It.'[59] This simple yet powerful message encapsulates the idea that success is often about taking the first step, regardless of the obstacles or the outcome.

The story behind Nike's slogan is a celebration of not just the champions and winners but also the everyday people who have the courage to lace up their shoes, step out the door and start pursuing their dreams. These are the people who wake up early, push themselves beyond their comfort zones and keep going, even when the going gets tough. They are the embodiment of determination, resilience and the power of taking action.

Small good deeds are better than the greatest good intentions. Every journey begins with a single step. Take the first step towards your goals, no matter how big or small. Embrace the spirit of Nike's slogan and remember that progress is made not by standing still but by taking action, learning from mistakes and continuously pushing forward. Don't worry about how quick you are or who's watching you, just do it!

Traction requires consistent action

It takes clarity, confidence and courage to make bold decisions, and commitment and consistent action to follow through to the desired outcome. Achieving traction in your personal and professional lives is all about taking consistent, purposeful action. As Gino Wickman explains in his book, *Traction*,[60] traction is the result of focusing on the right activities, setting clear goals and holding yourself accountable to make continuous progress. He goes on to say, 'Vision without traction is merely hallucination.'

Consistent action creates momentum and propels you forward, even when faced with challenges or setbacks. It's the driving force that keeps you moving towards your goals and helps you stay on track. By regularly evaluating your actions and adjusting your approach, you can ensure that your activities align with your objectives and contribute to your overall success.

You can achieve anything you set your mind to when you follow a plan that works and take consistent daily action. To achieve traction in your life, commit to making steady progress each day. Identify the high-impact activities that will drive your success and develop a plan to consistently work on them. By doing so, you'll build momentum, stay focused on your goals and ultimately achieve them faster.

One of the main reasons I see people holding back is self-doubt. Alex Hormozi, entrepreneur and author of the book, *$100M Offers*, says you must 'out-work your self-doubt'.[61] I couldn't agree more. Consistent action will build your competence and confidence, as we discussed earlier in this book. You've got to get in the reps if you want to build strength in any area of your life or business.

With clarity, courage and consistent action, you'll overcome your fears and build momentum towards your goals to achieve a life of significance and impact. Without consistent action, your dreams and aspirations will remain elusive.

I listened to Denzel Washington delivering a speech once, where he said, 'Dreams without action, are just dreams ... Without commitment, you'll never start but without consistency, you'll never finish.'[62] Consistency is key.

So, how do you establish consistent action? How do you build momentum? It all comes down to the power of routine.

The power of routines to build momentum

Routines, rituals, rhythms... they have a warm familiarity about them. We find comfort in their steady consistency. These patterns provide a sense of structure and stability in our lives, allowing us to navigate the ebb and flow of daily challenges with greater ease. Embracing routines helps us build a strong foundation for personal and professional growth, enabling us to reach our goals and achieve success.

In his book, *The Compound Effect*,[63] Darren Hardy teaches us about the power of small, consistent actions over time and how they can lead to significant results in various aspects of life, including personal development, relationships, health and finances. Small everyday choices and habits compound over time, leading to massive results, whether positive or negative.

Having routines in your personal life, and having good routines or meeting rhythms in your business, is like having a clear, solid drumbeat in a song – they provide a foundation that allows all the other elements to flourish harmoniously. Just as a kick drum establishes a steady, predictable beat that sets the tempo and underpins the rhythm for the entire band, effective routines and rhythms in your life and business create a structure that supports growth, productivity and success.

Imagine a song without a drumbeat; the other instruments would struggle to find their place, lacking the guidance and cohesion that comes from a strong rhythmic backbone. Similarly, without well-defined routines in your personal life or meeting rhythms in your business, the various components may falter or become disjointed, ultimately limiting your potential for progress and achievement. By establishing and maintaining solid routines, you create a dependable framework that enables you to navigate the complexities of life and business with greater ease and confidence.

Harnessing the power of momentum in your personal and professional lives is vital to achieving your goals and liberating your greatness. Sir Isaac Newton's first Law of Motion,[64] also known as the Law of Inertia, can be applied metaphorically to the concept of momentum in our lives. The law states that an object at rest will stay at rest, and an object in motion will stay in motion with a constant velocity, unless acted upon by an external force. In the context of personal development, this means that once you start taking action it becomes easier to maintain that forward progress, leading to a snowball effect of success.

Establishing daily, weekly, monthly, quarterly and annual routines is a powerful way to create and maintain momentum in your journey towards greatness. These routines provide structure, focus and consistency, ensuring that you stay on track and remain committed to your goals. Establishing and maintaining routines is a proven method for maximising productivity, increasing focus and facilitating personal and professional growth. By breaking down your objectives into manageable tasks and regularly reviewing your progress, you can continually adjust your strategies and make improvements.

There are five routines that my team and I practise in our own business, and that our clients use to achieve their goals. Implemented consistently every day, week, month and quarter, these routines will help you build unstoppable momentum.

Daily disciplines

Your daily routines lay the foundation for your success, as they help to cultivate habits that support your goals. Establishing consistent daily practices, such as exercise, meditation and setting priorities, ensures that you're continuously working towards achieving your objectives and maintaining a healthy work-life balance.

Your daily routine will help you bring presence, gratitude and energy to your day so that you can focus on your goals and actions required to move the needle forward. Your daily disciplines should also include five minutes at the end of each day to reflect on how you performed, so that you can continue or course correct the next day.

Every successful person will tell you that discipline created the structure and freedom for them to thrive. The objective of your daily disciplines is to get better every day.

Weekly WRAP

Weekly routines allow you to reflect on your achievements, identify areas for growth and plan for the upcoming week. Setting aside time each week to review your completed tasks, analyse your performance and determine areas where improvements can be made ensures that you stay focused and motivated. Additionally, weekly planning sessions help you allocate your time effectively, enhancing your productivity and work quality.

The method I teach for weekly routines is WRAP: weekly review and preview. Review your progress over the past week, celebrate and internalise your wins and appreciate the lessons learnt. By celebrating wins and lessons learnt, you'll take the momentum of the previous week into the next.

Preview the week ahead with the intention to learn, grow and focus on the needle movers. Determine your attitude and behaviour for the week ahead. What must you start, stop or continue thinking, feeling, believing or doing in the upcoming week? Also commit to game-changer actions or OTPs (one thing priorities – the must-do priorities to complete before the end of the week).

The objective with your weekly WRAP is to get better every week.

Monthly milestones

Monthly routines provide an opportunity to assess your progress over an extended period and recalibrate your strategies accordingly. This longer timeframe allows you to gain a more comprehensive understanding of your achievements and challenges, enabling you to make well-informed decisions about which goals and projects to prioritise.

Monthly reviews also serve as a valuable opportunity to celebrate your successes, fostering a sense of accomplishment and motivation. What you measure and monitor improves, so it's important to track and monitor key performance indicators to ensure good awareness, alignment and action.

The objective with your monthly milestones is to get better every month.

Quarterly quests

Quarterly routines offer a broader perspective, enabling you to evaluate your overall progress and set new targets for the upcoming quarter. These reviews give you a chance to revisit your long-term goals and ensure that your actions align with your overarching vision.

Quarterly routines also enable you to identify any emerging trends or market shifts that may impact your strategies, allowing you to adapt proactively and stay ahead of the competition.

The objective with your quarterly quests is to get better every quarter.

Annual aspirations

Annual routines serve as a powerful tool for reflection and strategic planning. They enable us to look back on the past year, celebrate our accomplishments, learn from our setbacks and set ambitious goals for the coming year.

By taking the time to analyse our performance and growth over the entire year, we can identify trends, adjust our long-term vision and create a detailed roadmap for future success. Annual routines also offer an opportunity to evaluate your personal and professional development, ensuring that you continue to grow and thrive in all aspects of your life.

The objective with your annual aspirations is to get better every year.

By consistently implementing daily, weekly, monthly, quarterly and annual routines, you can create a structure that accelerates your growth and helps you achieve your goals faster. These routines provide a framework for ongoing reflection, evaluation and adjustment, ensuring that you remain proactive and intentional in your pursuit of personal and professional success. By leveraging the power of routines, you can build unstoppable momentum, unlock your full potential and liberate your greatness.

Here are some of the key benefits of having good routines:

- Structure and organisation

- Habit formation

- Reduced decision fatigue

- Increased focus and discipline

- Enhanced work-life balance

- Greater consistency and reliability

- Better stress management

- Improved self-confidence

Develop routines that align with your objectives and commit to taking action. As you make progress, celebrate your wins – no matter how small – and use them as motivation to keep pushing forward.

There's no such thing as 'time management', only 'self-management'

I used to believe that there was not enough time in the day for me to achieve my goals and work through my never-ending to-do lists. Yet, time is the one resource that's equally distributed among all of us. How do some people achieve phenomenal success and others don't, when we all have the same 24 hours in a day, 7 days in a week and 365 days in a year? No one can truly manage time; it marches on relentlessly, no matter what we do.

There's no such thing as 'time management', only 'self-management'. We can't manage time, but we can manage ourselves in the time we have available. When I realised that I wasn't achieving my goals because I wasn't managing myself well, I studied goal-attainment theory and bought so many planners to help me. None of the planners fully resonated with me, so I created a *Success Journal* to help me gain greater clarity and purposeful direction. It's allowed me greater intentionality and productivity through better planning and preparation for each day, and laser focus on the needle-moving activities required to help me achieve my goals. That's where you'll find the daily, weekly, monthly and quarterly routines as part of my ninety-day success plan.

The strategies and frameworks in the *Success Journal* have worked for me and my clients, and I'm excited to see what you'll achieve using it, if you choose to do so. Whether you use the *Success Journal* or not, by improving your self-management skills, you will increase productivity, reduce stress, achieve a better work-life balance and improve your overall quality of life.

Mastering self-management is a journey, and like any skill it takes study and practice to improve. Keep working on these techniques, and soon you'll find that you're accomplishing more than you ever thought possible in the time you have available each day, week, month and year.

Summary

Remember that continuously taking deliberate, focused action will propel you towards your goals and, ultimately, your desired level of success. Embrace the power of action and never shy away from the opportunities and challenges that come your way. Maintain a mindset that focuses on progress over perfection and strive to learn from every experience.

By committing to the Principle of Action, taking consistent, courageous action, you'll be well on your way to liberating your greatness and making a lasting impact in your life and the lives of those around you. Your answer is always in your activity – that's the Principle of Action.

Practical application

Reflect on the Principle of Action

Reflection is a skill. Take a moment to capture your thoughts and commit to taking consistent action to move the needle forward.

- What key insights did you discover in this chapter?

- What decisions are you committed to making to gain the greatest return?

- What disciplined action will you take in the next week/month/quarter that will give you the greatest reward?

Activity

In the spirit of striving for excellence and continual improvement, what will you...

STOP
(Doing / thinking
/ believing / feeling)

START
(Doing / thinking
/ believing / feeling)

CONTINUE
(Doing / thinking
/ believing / feeling)

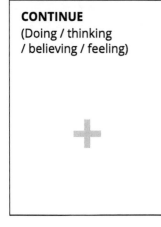

LEARN
(Book / online course
/ audio)

Additional resources

For bonus videos and downloadable content related to the Principle of Action, visit: www.liberateyourgreatness.com/action.

SIX

The Principle Of Accountability

Raise your standards for extraordinary results

Accountability is a vital component of the Liberating Greatness Framework, as it encourages a sense of ownership and responsibility in the pursuit of your goals. In this chapter, we will delve into the importance of holding yourself and others accountable, and how this can lead to raising your standards for extraordinary results. We will also explore various tools and techniques that can help you build a culture of accountability, both personally and professionally, fostering an environment where everyone is committed to achieving their best. But before we get into what you need to know about accountability...

How do you feel about accountability?

Accountability is an interesting principle because not everyone sees it as a positive concept. It might be a word that instils a sense of discomfort, as it often carries with it the weight of responsibility and the possibility of consequences. Not everyone wants to be held accountable.

Accountability is an essential component of personal and professional growth, and embracing it can lead to incredible progress and success. My goal for this chapter is to help you see the benefits of accountability in your life and inspire you to harness its powerful drive to achieve even greater results.

After diligently cultivating heightened awareness, achieving greater alignment and taking positive action, accountability serves as another critical element in the Liberating Greatness Framework. It solidifies your commitment to personal and professional growth, ensuring that you consistently strive for excellence and remain focused on your objectives. Accountability is the driving force that challenges you to turn your aspirations into tangible accomplishments and propels you towards liberating your greatness.

Accountability is the willingness to take ownership of your actions, your decisions and their outcomes. It involves acknowledging your role in the results you achieve – whether they are positive or negative – and using that understanding to learn, grow and improve. By adopting an attitude of accountability, you demonstrate integrity, trustworthiness and a commitment to continuous development.

What would your life look like if you didn't have to be responsible for your actions, your decisions and their outcomes? It may seem like a tempting proposition at first, free from the constraints of expectations and consequences. However, this lack of responsibility would likely lead to a life of complacency, stagnation and unfulfilled potential. In a world without accountability, we would miss out on opportunities for personal growth, self-improvement and the satisfaction of achieving our goals. Our aspirations would fade into the background as we would have little motivation to push beyond our comfort zones, challenge ourselves or strive for greatness. Ultimately, it is our responsibility for our actions, our decisions and their outcomes that fuels our progress, ignites our passions and empowers us to live purposeful, meaningful lives.

You'll always do more for your coach, team or family than for yourself

For a couple of years, my friend and I ran an online fitness programme in which people from various countries, diverse backgrounds and all shapes and sizes embarked on a ninety-day challenge. Day by day, we coached them on mindset, nutrition and exercise. Participants were required to submit photos of their meals, weekly body images and video proof of their completed exercise challenges. We celebrated those making the effort every week in our Facebook groups.

From the first engagement with participants, we urged them to 'stick to the plan' if they wanted to see results. Those who lacked the discipline to stick to the plan, gradually dropped out. However, those who reached the thirty-day milestone, then the sixty-day milestone and ultimately crossed the finish line on the ninetieth day achieved phenomenal results. Upon revealing the body transformations, an overwhelming sense of euphoria swept over everyone involved. They had achieved what they set out to achieve, and what's more, they discovered a new-found inner strength and belief that anything was possible…

When the euphoria settled down a day or two later, panic started to set in as nutrition became a little more relaxed and exercise discipline dwindled. Why? Because we were no longer holding them accountable. The food cravings may have gone, but now they were craving accountability. No one was watching anymore, so people went off the rails a little.

Adapting the programmes – and to avoid participants becoming dependent on us – we included new training on how to sustain their results beyond the ninety days and encouraged community support to keep each other accountable. When people are watching you, you're more likely to stick to the plan.

As you read this book or participate in any of my liberating greatness coaching programmes, you'll notice that my aim is not to create a dependency on me as your coach but rather to encourage you to rely on the Principle of Accountability to help you achieve your goals.

When someone is holding you accountable, you will:

- Follow through on your commitments

- Do the right thing, with clarity, conviction and courage

- Prioritise and manage yourself effectively in the time you have available

- Reflect on your progress regularly

- Learn from your setbacks and use them as setups for growth

- Get better and improve

- Stay motivated and committed to your goals

- Develop a stronger sense of self-discipline

- Build resilience and adaptability in the face of challenges

- Foster a sense of responsibility for your own success, well-being and relationships

By embracing accountability, you empower yourself to take control of your life and unlock your full potential on your journey towards greatness. What might you achieve in the next ninety days if you had an accountability partner or coach holding you to higher standards? In the spirit of acknowledging both the ROI and COI, what if you don't have anyone in your corner cheering you on and holding you accountable?

The impact of the absence of accountability at work

Imagine a workplace where nobody takes responsibility for their actions or the results they produce. It's a scenario that can quickly spiral into chaos, leading to a host of detrimental consequences for individuals, teams and organisations. The negative effects that can arise when accountability is lacking in the workplace are:

- **Lack of ownership** – When individuals or teams fail to take responsibility for their actions and outcomes a lack of ownership prevails. This can lead to finger pointing, blame shifting and an overall unwillingness to address issues or problems that arise.

- **Decreased motivation** – Without accountability, people may not feel a sense of urgency or commitment to achieving their goals. This can lead to decreased motivation, as there are no clear consequences or rewards tied to success or failure.

- **Poor performance** – In an environment where accountability is lacking, performance standards may slip as individuals and teams become less driven to excel. This can result in lower-quality work, missed deadlines and unmet goals.

- **Stunted growth** – When people are not held accountable for their actions and outcomes, opportunities for personal and professional growth may be limited. Without the impetus to learn from mistakes and improve, individuals may stagnate and fail to reach their full potential.

- **Damaged relationships** – A lack of accountability can strain relationships between team members, as trust and respect can be eroded when people fail to own their actions and their consequences. This can create a toxic environment where collaboration and teamwork suffer.

- **Hindered progress** – When accountability is absent, progress towards goals and objectives can be slow or non-existent. This can have significant repercussions for individuals, teams and organisations, as opportunities for success may be missed or squandered.

- **Diminished credibility** – A persistent lack of accountability can damage an individual's or organisation's credibility and reputation. Over time, this can lead to a loss of trust from clients, partners or stakeholders, as well as reduced confidence from team members.

If you're reading through the consequences above and recognising some of those manifesting in your workplace, chances are it's due to a lack of accountability. To prevent these negative consequences, it's essential to cultivate a culture of accountability in both personal and professional settings. By taking responsibility for our actions and their outcomes, we can foster an environment where individuals and teams can thrive, grow and achieve their goals.

Cultivating a culture of accountability

Remember that mastery takes time; transformation takes time. Be sure to communicate well and include your people in discussing, accepting and embracing the following guiding principles for cultivating a culture of accountability:

- **Accountability is a choice** – Cultivating a culture of accountability starts with a conscious decision to take ownership of your actions, your decisions and their outcomes. It's a commitment to growth and personal responsibility that can lead to increased success and satisfaction in all aspects of life.

- **Accountability builds trust** – When you demonstrate accountability, you show that you are reliable and can be counted on to keep your word. This helps build trust and credibility with your peers, colleagues or team members, fostering stronger relationships and more effective collaboration.

- **Accountability promotes learning** – Holding yourself accountable creates opportunities for learning and improvement. By reflecting on your experiences and evaluating your actions, you can identify areas for growth and development, which can ultimately lead to better results and increased personal and professional success.

- **Accountability drives performance** – A culture of accountability can inspire higher levels of performance, as individuals recognise the importance of owning their actions and achieving their goals. This can lead to increased motivation, focus and determination, ultimately driving better results for individuals and organisations alike.

- **Accountability is empowering** – Taking ownership of your actions and their outcomes gives you a sense of control over your life and future. By embracing accountability, you empower yourself to make choices, learn from your experiences and shape the course of your personal and professional journey.

- **Accountability is a shared responsibility** – While it's important to hold yourself accountable, it's equally essential to create an environment where others feel encouraged to do the same. Encourage a culture of accountability within your team or organisation by promoting open communication, setting clear expectations and providing constructive feedback.

- **Accountability requires self-reflection** – To truly embrace accountability, you must be willing to engage in self-reflection and honestly assess your actions and their outcomes. This introspection can help you better understand your strengths and weaknesses, enabling you to grow and develop as an individual.

- **Accountability encourages transparent performance metrics** – Transparent performance metrics provide a clear, objective way to measure progress and hold yourself and your team members accountable for their results. By tracking and sharing these metrics, you enable your team to see the impact of their efforts and understand how they contribute to the organisation's success.

- **Accountability enhances self-awareness** – By holding yourself accountable, or being held accountable by others, you become more in tune with your actions, thoughts and emotions. This heightened self-awareness is key to your personal growth and transformation. As you now know, all proactive change starts with awareness.

Understanding and cultivating a culture of accountability can be a powerful catalyst for growth and success in your personal and professional lives. By taking ownership of your actions, your decisions and their outcomes, learning from your experiences and fostering a culture of responsibility, you can unlock your full potential to help you achieve greatness.

Who's holding you accountable?

When people are depending on you to show up on your A-game and deliver your best, the Principle of

Accountability will challenge and push you to be more, do more, achieve more and give more. So, who's holding you accountable? There are four levels of accountability:

Level 1: Accountability to yourself

The buck stops with you. Personal accountability demonstrates you have an internal locus of control versus blaming others, which is an external locus of control. To cultivate accountability to yourself, implement everything we've covered in this book so far: seek greater awareness and alignment, consistently take massive action and constantly evaluate your progress. Being accountable to yourself means being honest about your successes and failures and taking responsibility for your actions and their outcomes.

When you demonstrate personal accountability, you send a message to the world that you are confident and courageous. You're prepared to back yourself, take action and then take responsibility for the consequences. That displays a high level of integrity and vulnerability – both of which are attractive. People want to work with those who exude integrity and have the inner strength to be publicly vulnerable.

In my teams, I want my people to trust that I will honour them when they take personal responsibility and accountability for their actions. Even when they've messed up, if they take ownership we'll work through it together. I'll respect them for making the effort and we'll appreciate the learning moments.

When I'm coaching corporate teams, I can see future leaders emerge when they take personal responsibility and accountability for their actions, decisions and results. They are the future leaders, leading by example, raising their hand when they've messed up, learning, growing, breaking through barriers and exceeding expectations. They also get promoted faster than their peers because they can be trusted to own their role and area of responsibility passionately.

By contrast, I've seen people not take accountability for their poor performance or results who have ended up leaving or being asked to leave the business. When I see people blaming others or their circumstances and not taking responsibility and accountability for their own actions, it's a red flag that they may need to move on.

Recognise that you're here for a reason: to bring your purpose, mission, vision and values to life and make a positive, significant impact on all those around you. Embracing this level of accountability requires you to be honest with yourself and to truly examine your motivations and aspirations. As you do, you'll discover that your sense of purpose can become a guiding force, directing your actions and decisions. You can create a life of meaning and significance that goes far beyond the pursuit of personal success. Use your time, talent and treasure to be the best you can be with all you've been given.

There's a powerful ten times two-letter word mantra I'd encourage you to embrace that will bring this level of accountability to life: 'If it is to be, it is up to me.' Take responsibility for your past, your present and your future. Hold yourself accountable, and I know you will achieve extraordinary results, personally and professionally.

Level 2: Accountability to your family

Your immediate and extended family often serves as your primary support system, and being accountable to them is essential for maintaining strong relationships and creating a nurturing environment. Family can play a pivotal role in keeping you focused, motivated and committed to achieving your goals, especially if they're dependent on you. To strengthen accountability to your family, follow the steps below:

- **Establish shared goals** – Work together as a family to create common goals that align with individual aspirations and priorities. This collaborative approach fosters unity, mutual understanding and shared commitment to success.

- **Schedule regular check-ins** – Set aside time to discuss your progress, challenges and achievements with your family members. These conversations can help you stay on track, celebrate milestones and address any obstacles that may arise.

- **Provide and seek feedback** – Encourage open and honest dialogue within your family, allowing for constructive criticism and feedback to help you grow and improve. In return, offer guidance and support to your family members in their pursuits.

- **Acknowledge and appreciate efforts** – Recognise the efforts and accomplishments of your family members as they work towards their goals. Show gratitude for their support and encouragement, and express your pride in their achievements.

- **Model accountability** – Demonstrate your commitment to accountability by holding yourself to high standards and consistently taking responsibility for your actions. Your example will inspire your family members to do the same.

- **Foster a growth mindset** – Cultivate an environment that encourages learning, exploration and personal development for all family members. Emphasise the importance of resilience, adaptability and perseverance in the face of challenges.

- **Balance personal and family responsibilities** – Be mindful of the impact your personal goals and commitments may have on your family life. Strive to maintain a healthy balance between individual pursuits and family obligations and be willing to adapt and adjust as needed.

I'm accountable to my wife and my kids. I want them to hold me accountable, and what's more, I *need* them to hold me accountable. They're why I do what I do. If I lose my sense of accountability to them, I lose the necessity to show up every day and bring my purpose to life, for them and all those around me. They are 100% worth fighting for and they inspire me daily to be better. I want to be a role model for my kids. They hold me to a higher standard.

By being accountable to your family, you demonstrate that you value their support and are dedicated to fulfilling your responsibilities to them. Strive to be a role model for your family by embracing personal growth and development and encouraging them to do the same.

Level 3: Accountability to your accountability partners

A kite rises against the wind, not with the wind. Like wind beneath our wings, we need the challenge and push from others to lift us up to greater heights. That could come in the form of competitors, team members, coaches, masterminds and inner-circle friends. While your competition won't directly hold you accountable, you can use their activity in the marketplace to push you to get better, by becoming more, doing more and achieving more. Consider the power of intentionally lining up your accountability partners, in the form of your team, coaches, masterminds and inner-circle friends:

- **Team** – Your team members are a crucial part of your support system, and they rely on you as much as you rely on them. By holding each other accountable for your actions, decisions and results, you can create a collaborative environment that fosters growth, development and success. Encourage open communication and mutual support among your team and celebrate each other's accomplishments.

- **Coaches** – A coach can be an invaluable asset in helping you stay accountable and on track to achieve your goals. By providing guidance, feedback and encouragement, a coach can help you identify your strengths and weaknesses, overcome obstacles and make progress towards your objectives. Engage regularly with your coach and be open to their suggestions and recommendations.

- **Masterminds** – Mastermind groups bring together like-minded individuals who are committed to supporting one another in their personal and professional endeavours. By participating in a mastermind group, you gain access to a network of peers who can offer diverse perspectives, ideas and experiences, as well as hold you accountable to your commitments. Regularly attend mastermind meetings, share your goals and challenges, and actively contribute to the success of others in the group.

- **Inner-circle friends** – Inner-circle friends are the irreplaceable threads in the fabric of our lives. These trusted allies go beyond professional bonds and step into deep, personal, emotional and spiritual territory. They are the select few you can call on at any hour and who will offer a listening ear, honest feedback and heartfelt encouragement. These friends understand your dreams and ambitions. They are there to catch you during stumbles, and they will celebrate your victories and remind you of your potential in times of doubt. They are not simply yes-men; they serve as mirrors, reflecting your strengths and weaknesses to keep you grounded and focused. Share your goals, challenges and progress with your inner-circle friends and reciprocate their support. Remember, a powerful inner circle thrives on mutual respect and reciprocity. I'm especially grateful to Shaun Lewarne and Arthur Stamatis for their devoted inner-circle friendships over more than two decades. They've helped me through some of the toughest moments in my life, and we've celebrated many 'Moët moments' together.

My team, coaches, masterminds and inner-circle friends have been key ingredients in my success to date, and they'll be key ingredients in my future, too. They're there for me through ups and downs. They inspire, encourage, challenge and push me to achieve incredible things.

For almost twenty-five years, I've invested so much of my time, energy and money in my own learning and development in the form of online courses, coaching and masterminds. By far, the fastest ways I've learnt to achieve my goals is having expert coaches guide, challenge and push me; mastermind accountability partners, where we contribute to each other's businesses as if they're our own; and team members whom I know are counting on me to support them in providing for their families.

I will say, not all of my coaches in the past have been great, but I always learnt at least one thing from them that could help me or help someone else, so I've seen that as a worthwhile experience. Some of my coaches have been absolute game-changers in my life. So, if you're looking to hire a coach, be discerning in your selection.

Having a coach or actively participating in a mastermind can be transformative in your personal and professional lives, guiding you towards growth, success and self-improvement, with benefits including:

- **Clarity and focus** – A coach helps you see the bigger picture and gain clarity on your goals, values and priorities, enabling you to develop a clear vision for your life and career. By understanding what truly matters to you, you can focus your energy and resources on the activities that bring you closer to your objectives.

- **Congruence and accountability** – One of the most significant benefits of having a coach is the increased sense of accountability. A coach holds you responsible for your actions and progress, ensuring that you stay committed to your goals, even when the going gets tough. This level of accountability can greatly improve your chances of success.

- **Considered, personalised guidance** – A good coach tailors their approach to your unique needs, strengths and challenges. They provide customised advice and strategies that are specifically designed to help you overcome obstacles, break through limiting beliefs, instil confidence and create a roadmap for success, making the most of your potential.

- **Competence and skill development** – A coach can identify areas where you need improvement and provide targeted training to help you develop new skills and enhance existing ones. This can lead to better performance, increased confidence and greater overall satisfaction in your personal and professional lives.

- **Camaraderie and emotional support** – A coach is not only a source of practical advice but also a trusted confidant who can provide emotional support during challenging times. They can help you navigate difficult emotions, such as fear, doubt and frustration, and keep you motivated to persevere in the face of adversity. Especially if you're in a leadership role, you need a professional with whom you can talk through your ideas, brainstorm options, and get creative in addressing problems and finding solutions.

- **Composed, unbiased perspective** – As an objective third party, a coach can offer unbiased insights and feedback that friends, family or colleagues may not be able to provide. This impartial perspective can help you see situations more clearly, make better decisions and address blind spots that you might not have been aware of.

- **Calm, non-judgemental input** – Great coaches are non-judgemental. They see you for who you are and who you want to be as the best version of yourself. They will call you out on limiting beliefs and negative behaviours, and they'll do it in a non-judgemental, supportive and encouraging way.

- **Challenge and accelerated growth** – By leveraging the expertise and guidance of a coach, you can achieve your goals more quickly and efficiently than you would on your own. Coaches can share proven techniques, best practices and shortcuts that can save you time, effort and potential setbacks.

The power of coaching

The journey towards greatness is often a challenging one, and having a coach by your side can make all the difference. A coach can be an invaluable investment in your personal and professional development. Their support, guidance and expertise can help you navigate challenges, develop new skills and achieve your goals faster than you might have thought possible. By having a coach hold you accountable, you gain a crucial ally in your pursuit of greatness; someone who is genuinely invested in your success.

If you think about any sports professional, you'll notice that they have a coach (potentially a team of coaches) in their corner. Even Tiger Woods has a team of coaches around him. Think about that, the best golfer in the world still needs to be coached. Throughout his professional career, Woods has primarily worked with three renowned swing coaches: Butch Harmon, Hank Haney and Sean Foley (additionally, he has worked with Chris Como as a swing consultant). He has also had other specialists on his team, including fitness trainers, mental coaches and physiotherapists. These professionals have played essential roles in maintaining his physical and mental well-being, helping him perform at the highest level.

Every athlete, every sports team will have a team of coaches. They understand the power of coaching in helping them accelerate their growth and achieve their goals faster. Having a great business coach and performance coach in your corner is one of the best investments you can make in the future of your business, career and life.

I have personally invested so much time, energy and money, learning from over forty coaches across various disciplines. Coaching is one of the fastest ways to accelerate your growth, learn the right strategies and frameworks, and avoid common mistakes on your journey to success.

The magic of masterminds

Masterminds provide an incredible opportunity to engage with people on a similar journey to you, often facing the same challenges and opportunities. Shared challenges lead to shared solutions. Masterminds bring together ambitious and driven people, all focused on achieving their goals and making a meaningful impact in their personal and professional lives. They can help you reach new heights, providing the support, accountability and inspiration needed to achieve new levels of success.

The magic of masterminds lies in the diverse experiences and perspectives of their members, and the unique structure which encourages collaboration, growth and deep connections. By bringing together individuals with diverse backgrounds, skills and perspectives, masterminds provide a dynamic environment where creativity flourishes and breakthrough ideas are born. This collective wisdom can help you overcome challenges, discover new opportunities and take your success to the next level much faster than if you were to struggle through your challenges on your own.

I've participated in some great and some not-so-good masterminds, so I've seen what works well and what doesn't. In the spirit of driving action and accountability, I ensure the masterminds I lead always focus on four main questions that everyone needs to prepare for each session:

1. What wins have you achieved over the past month?

2. What are you currently working on?

3. What help do you need to accelerate your growth?

4. What commitments are you making to stop/start/ continue/learn for the upcoming month?

Depending on the responses to these four questions, mastermind members offer support by providing information on systems and processes, sales and marketing strategies, perspective, positive challenge and encouragement.

Those four questions drive massive action, and our members make significant progress both in and between our sessions. Personally, I never want to show up to a mastermind where I'm not ready to share wins and updates on what I'm working on, which means that I do whatever I need to do between sessions to create those wins. Success begets success. One positive action after the next leads to progress, and consistent progress builds unstoppable momentum.

I also want to ensure I'm ready to contribute positively to other members in the group with any challenges they're having or help they may need. The best way to get the most out of a mastermind is to give the most to the mastermind. If everyone contributes at their highest levels, your mastermind will create a significant, positive impact for everyone involved.

In addition to driving action and accountability, I get energised by mastermind members sharing ideas, cheering each other on and creating deep, lasting relationships. Some of my closest friendships and success partnerships were formed in masterminds. They've challenged, inspired and encouraged me to level up my own thinking, and given me an opportunity to contribute to their growth in a meaningful way.

By leveraging the power of accountability partners in the form of your team, coaches and mastermind groups, you can cultivate a strong support network that drives you towards your goals and helps you rise to new heights. If you want to engage with accountability partners that will help you reach higher levels of success, I would like to invite you to join one of my coaching programmes, or my inner circle mastermind. Go to www.liberateyourgreatness.com/accountability for more information on how to apply.

Level 4: Accountability to your calling and your creator

Accountability is not only about being answerable to yourself and to others but also about being accountable to a higher purpose – your calling – and your reason for being here on this earth. When you align your actions with your greater mission, you ignite a powerful force within that compels you to stay true to your path, even in the face of challenges.

For me, this sense of accountability is deeply connected to my faith and belief that God has filled me with a desire to impact people positively and liberate greatness. It's why I do what I do. My commitment to fulfilling this purpose keeps me focused, inspired and driven to make a difference in the lives of others.

When your time on this earth ends, will you hear the words, 'Well done, good and faithful servant'?[65] That's one of the most challenging statements that I think about often, because I want to use my talents to their full potential. Although I find myself constantly falling short of my own expectations, at the same time I'm grateful for God's love, mercy and grace, and for another day to give it another go.

There's a wonderful story about when Michelangelo was working tirelessly on the Sistine Chapel's ceiling, high above the ground on a scaffold. A curious onlooker gazed up at the magnificent masterpiece he was creating. Astonished by the intricate details Michelangelo was painstakingly painting, the onlooker couldn't help but shout, 'Why so much detail? No one will be able to see that from down here!'

Michelangelo smiled and replied, 'God will see.'[66] His response beautifully illustrates his deep sense of accountability to God and dedication to his craft. He understood that his work was not just for the eyes of those who would view it from below but also for his creator. His commitment to excellence and attention to detail were manifestations of his personal responsibility and artistic integrity. This story is a powerful reminder that we, too, should strive to hold ourselves to higher standards and give our best effort in all that we do.

This story gives me such a wonderful sense of peace that I don't need to worry about what others think of me, my craft or the way I'm doing things. Provided I know that I've given my best and that 'God will see', I'm good.

Diamonds are formed under pressure

Let's take a moment to consider the process of how diamonds are formed. They begin as simple carbon atoms, buried deep within the earth. Over time, these atoms are subjected to incredible heat and pressure, and under these harsh conditions something remarkable happens. The carbon atoms bond together to form a crystal structure, and eventually, over millions of years, a diamond is born.

The diamond formation process is a perfect metaphor for our journey towards personal and professional greatness. Just like diamonds, we too are shaped and moulded by the pressures and challenges we face. When you commit to the levels of accountability outlined in this chapter – to yourself, your family, your team, coaches or masterminds, and ultimately to your calling and creator – you're consciously placing yourself in an environment designed for growth and transformation. This environment – this accountability – is the heat and pressure that helps you convert potential into performance.

Embracing these levels of accountability might feel uncomfortable or challenging at times, much like the intense heat and pressure the diamond must endure. Embrace the pressure. After all, it's under pressure that we, too, are transformed, refined and shaped from simple carbon into diamonds – resilient, brilliant and invaluable. This is a vital element of the journey to liberating your greatness.

Summary

Now that you know more about the benefits and power of accountability, and you have more clarity on who's holding you accountable, I'm going to ask you the same question I asked at the beginning of this chapter: How do you feel about accountability?

Are you feeling condemned or inspired? I hope it's the latter, because we are all works in progress, and accountability is a powerful way to help us move the needle forward and achieve greatness in all areas of our lives. In fact, I hope that you embrace accountability because of the opportunities it provides for greater connection, empowerment, confidence and encouragement on your quest for personal and professional success.

As we wrap up this chapter on the Principle of Accountability, reflect on the value of embracing responsibility and ownership in every aspect of your life.

Recognise the power that comes from being accountable to yourself, your family, your accountability partners and your creator. Keep in mind that accountability can be a driving force that pushes you to new heights, propelling you towards greater success and significance.

By cultivating a culture of accountability and surrounding yourself with people who share this commitment, you will be well equipped to face challenges head-on and liberate your greatness, making a lasting impact on the world. Nothing challenges you to level up more than accountability. Hold yourself to higher standards for extraordinary results – that's the Principle of Accountability.

Practical application

Reflect on the Principle of Accountability

Reflection is a skill. Take a moment to capture your thoughts and commit to taking consistent action to move the needle forward.

- What key insights did you discover in this chapter?

- What decisions are you committed to making to gain the greatest return?

- What disciplined action will you take in the next week/month/quarter that will give you the greatest reward?

Activity

In the spirit of striving for excellence and continual improvement, what will you...

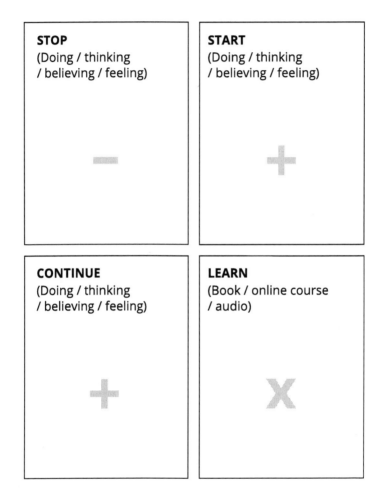

STOP
(Doing / thinking
/ believing / feeling)

START
(Doing / thinking
/ believing / feeling)

CONTINUE
(Doing / thinking
/ believing / feeling)

LEARN
(Book / online course
/ audio)

Additional resources

For bonus videos and downloadable content related to the Principle of Accountability, visit: www.liberateyourgreatness. com/accountability.

PART FOUR

IMPACT

In the final part of *Liberate Your Greatness*, we focus on the power of amplification and acceleration to create a lasting impact.

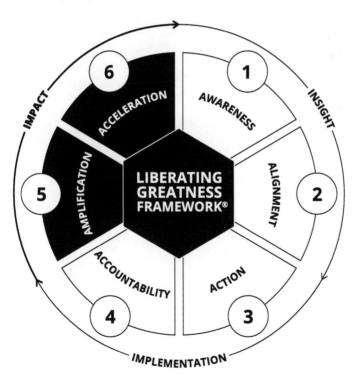

Building on the insight and implementation strategies from the previous sections, Part Four will guide you through the process of amplifying your influence, managing systems and leveraging your leadership skills to lead others in making a positive impact in the world.

As you explore Part Four, you'll discover how to harness the power of design thinking, innovation theory and the 0–1–100 framework to accelerate your growth and achieve extraordinary results. By mastering the art of amplification and acceleration, you'll be well on your way to creating a ripple effect of success, inspiring others to embrace their greatness, and leaving a legacy.

SEVEN

The Principle Of Amplification

Lead people, manage systems and use your influence to amplify your impact

The Principle of Amplification focuses on maximising your impact and influence, both as an individual and as a leader. To amplify, you need a magnifying glass, a catalyst or an amplifier that can take your existing potential and multiply its effectiveness, reaching new heights and touching more lives.

In this chapter, we will explore strategies and techniques that can help you amplify your efforts, making the most of your time, resources and energy. We will delve into the importance of effectively leading people, efficiently managing systems, and leveraging your influence and strategic partnerships to achieve more significant results. By understanding the power of amplification, you will be able to inspire and empower others, creating a ripple effect that extends far beyond your immediate circle of influence.

Before you turn up the volume, make sure you sound good

As a singer and acoustic guitarist, I love being in front of a microphone with my guitar plugged in and sound check done, ready to sing and play my heart out – when I'm well prepared. When I'm not well prepared, however, I consciously dial back the levels on my guitar, hoping that people won't hear it, let alone hear the mistakes I'm making. I'm a good enough vocalist to wing my singing, but there's no chance of me winging guitar chords I haven't learnt or practised repeatedly. I'm just not that good a musician.

It is important to get the first four steps of the Liberating Greatness Framework right before you try to amplify your impact. If you're clunky on the first four – if you lack awareness and are misaligned, taking the wrong action without the right levels of accountability – and you turn up the volume, you'll amplify noise rather than a beautifully orchestrated song. If your people are thinking and behaving badly, treating each other with disrespect, you'll amplify a toxic culture. If you haven't done the work behind closed doors, you'll either lack the confidence to perform in public, or worse – you'll lack the awareness that you are ill prepared and shouldn't be performing in public in the first place! If that's the case, you've missed an opportunity to positively amplify your impact, because you weren't ready for when the moment arrived.

Conversely, if you've been studying and practising in private – if you've done the work behind closed doors – what you amplify in public will have a positive impact. Amplification to create a bigger, even more positive impact comes when you've mastered steps one to four. Only then will you get to cascade your positive influence throughout your organisation and achieve greater results through your people.

Why would you want to amplify your impact?

Jim Rohn once said, 'The purpose of this human adventure is productivity. To see what all we can do with all we have been given.'[67]

Intuitively, I know that you're here reading this book because, deep inside, you know that you have more to give. You want to make an even bigger contribution to your family, your business and the world. To give more, you must first become more, do more and have more to give.

I also know how invested you are in your own learning and development, so that you have more to offer the world around you. This process of growth – liberating your greatness – is an ongoing journey; one that requires commitment, persistence, and a willingness to embrace challenges and learn from setbacks.

By amplifying your impact, you are effectively harnessing your unique gifts and abilities to create positive change in the world around you. In doing so, you not only improve the lives of those you touch, but also inspire them to strive for their own greatness. Maximising your impact and influence enables you to leave a legacy; one that will resonate with future generations and inspire them to follow in your footsteps. It allows you to tap into your full potential, stretching the boundaries of what you thought was possible and reaching for new heights of success and fulfilment.

In our fast-paced, interconnected world, your impact has the potential to spread rapidly, touching the lives of countless individuals across the globe. As you amplify your influence, you also create opportunities for collaboration, fostering a sense of unity and shared purpose among those who share your vision.

By continually striving to expand your impact and influence, you are setting a powerful example for others to follow. You demonstrate that it is possible to create meaningful change and that each person has the potential to make a difference, no matter how small their initial sphere of influence may seem. Isn't that what we should all be striving for as leaders – to create meaningful change?

In the 2000 film *Gladiator*,[68] directed by Ridley Scott, the protagonist Maximus Decimus Meridius, portrayed by Russell Crowe, is a Roman general who leads his troops into battle against the Germanic tribes. Before the battle commences, Maximus rallies and inspires his soldiers with a rousing speech. As the soldiers gather around him, preparing for the upcoming conflict, Maximus confidently proclaims, 'What we do in life echoes in eternity.'

I'm a sucker for epic battle scenes, and this is one of those memorable lines that emphasises the importance and lasting impact of our actions, not only in our own lives or the lives of those close to us, but also on the greater course of history. Our actions, decisions and choices leave a legacy, transcending time and influencing future generations. Maximus's words serve as a reminder that what we do today can continue to reverberate long after we are gone, inspiring us to make a meaningful and positive impact in the world.

That's what I want for my own life, and for yours. Legacy. Amplified impact. That long after we're gone and people no longer remember our names, people recognise that someone, at some point in history, made a positive decision, took courageous action and made a meaningful impact that changed the course of their future.

We have that opportunity every day. At work – on the battlefield, so to speak – and at home. One of my clients had a breakthrough insight in our session on mindset, mastering our psychology, when he realised the negative impact he was having at home with one of his daughters. He was upset about having gone into his daughter's room after finishing a long day at work, to call her for dinner, and upon seeing her room being messy, he said to her, 'This is unacceptable, tidy up your room immediately!'

She responded, 'Nice to see you too, Dad, how was your day?' He felt gutted! Guiding him to create a new belief about the potential positive impact he could have by being more patient and intentional in future, I helped him realise that he had the ability to positively influence the environment. His new belief is: 'My ability to positively influence the environment is a superpower.' He now reminds himself of that every time he engages with his daughter and it has enhanced the way they communicate and connect. He positively influences his environment at work, too.

How do you amplify your impact? You turn up the volume through people, systems and your influence. More specifically, you amplify your impact through leading people, managing systems and using your influence for good. By mastering these elements, you will be well equipped to make a lasting, positive impact that extends far beyond your immediate sphere of influence.

With this foundation in place, let's explore each of these areas in more detail, beginning with effective leadership.

Amplify your impact by leading people

There are many characteristics of effective leaders. We should all have a common goal and that is to connect, inspire, encourage and uplift our people. Effective leaders possess a range of qualities that enable them to guide their teams towards success. These characteristics include: clear communication, integrity, empathy, resilience and adaptability.

Strong leaders are also able to articulate a compelling vision for their organisation, set goals and create a culture of collaboration. Mastering the Principles of Awareness, Alignment, Action and Accountability will enable you to embody these traits and foster an environment in which your team members feel supported, valued and empowered to reach their full potential.

Business is, and always will be, about people dealing with people. Creating an environment of trust, connection, rapport, empathy and understanding is essential for fostering strong relationships, which is paramount in effective leadership. By fostering a culture where team members feel valued, respected and supported, leaders can cultivate a sense of belonging and collaboration within the organisation.

The foundation of trust

Relationships are built on a foundation of trust, which is a critical component in any interaction. Trust has two key aspects: being trusting of others and being trustworthy. One is your gift to others; the other is earned.

Being trusting of others means having faith in their abilities, intentions and reliability. By demonstrating trust in your team members, you create an environment where they feel empowered to take risks, share ideas and collaborate effectively.

On the other hand, being trustworthy is about consistently exhibiting integrity, honesty and dependability. As a leader, your actions and decisions should reflect your commitment to keeping promises, being transparent and acting in the best interests of your team and organisation. When you are perceived as trustworthy, your team members are more likely to feel secure, confident and willing to follow your guidance.

This foundation of trust not only strengthens relationships among team members but also enhances their commitment, motivation and overall performance. By prioritising trust and nurturing genuine connections, you can amplify your impact and create a thriving, cohesive team that is well equipped to face challenges and achieve success together.

My first manager in the corporate world, Alistair Noyce, was a wonderful, inspiring and memorable leader. I had joined Procter & Gamble in Cape Town, South Africa, fresh out of university, and had the privilege of being led by Alistair. Apart from creating early opportunities for me to learn and grow, he taught me so many foundational principles that I've continued to implement in my professional life. One of them was about trust.

He walked over to my desk one day, briefed me on a project he wanted me to lead, and then held up a standard HB pencil in front of me. He said, 'I trust you, John. Trust is like this lead pencil. If you break trust, it's very difficult to restore,' to which he dramatically snapped the pencil in half. He continued, 'Even if you put these two pieces together again, tape it up, and try to write with it, the lead in the centre will always be broken. Don't snap the pencil!'

That message has always stuck with me. Can you imagine how much more effective your team might be when together you agree principles to adhere to, and recognise the actions that might 'snap the pencil', with a commitment to each other to never 'snap the pencil'?

Effective leaders are inspiring and memorable because they build trust, rapport and relationship by instilling principles that last forever.

Develop your leadership style and empower your team

To amplify your impact as a leader, it is essential to develop a leadership style that aligns with your values and strengths and the unique needs of your organisation. If you're an experienced leader, you may already have your leadership style developed to a larger degree. My most senior corporate clients recognise they're always learning, always growing, always fine-tuning their leadership style. Think about how you might refine and enhance yours. If, on the other hand, you're a relatively new leader, developing your leadership style could take you weeks, months, even years to develop.

Whatever level you're at, there's another level for you to achieve. Start by reflecting on your natural leadership tendencies and identify areas where you may need to grow or adapt. Seek feedback from trusted colleagues, mentors or coaches to gain a deeper understanding of how your leadership style is perceived by others. By refining your leadership style and continuously striving to improve, you can create an environment in which your team members feel inspired, motivated and empowered to contribute to the organisation's success.

I have the privilege of coaching a thoughtful, engaging and inspirational leader, William, who has the humility to learn and grow despite over three decades of leading individuals and teams around the world. Part of his leadership philosophy is to 'lead, follow or get out of the way'. His purpose is to 'create an environment for people to thrive'. Sometimes that means he needs to lead the charge, sometimes he needs to follow or run alongside people for support, and other times he needs to get out of the way and let his people do and be their best.

Help the team to knock it out of the park

Coaches don't run onto the field to play for their team. They cheer from the sideline, call time outs when necessary, and keep individuals and the collective team focused and inspired. Then they trust the team to do what they're trained, equipped and empowered to do.

As a leader, one of your most important responsibilities is to train, equip and empower your team members. This involves creating opportunities for growth and learning, providing constructive feedback, and recognising and rewarding their efforts. By investing in the professional and personal development of your team members, you can help them to unlock their full potential and become more effective contributors to the organisation. Additionally, by demonstrating your commitment to their growth, you will build trust and loyalty, ultimately leading to a more engaged and energised team.

In Jim Collins' book *Good to Great*,[69] he speaks about 'Getting the right people on the bus, and the wrong people off the bus.' Both are important to ensure the bus goes in the right direction without having to constantly stop. One of the most significant factors in achieving success and liberating your greatness is the ability to amplify your impact through people. When you put the best people in the biggest opportunities, they'll achieve phenomenal results. By surrounding yourself with the right individuals and fostering a supportive, high-performing environment, you can create a synergistic effect that propels you and your team towards your goals.

Coaching C-suite executives and management teams means that I'm often involved in discussions about people, organisational designs and raising leaders for the future. During those conversations, I encourage my clients to consider the five rights:

1. The right people…

2. …on the right seats…

3. ...doing the right things...

4. ...at the right time...

5. ...with the right DNA.

All five are key to ensuring success for the individuals, teams and business, and developing a high-performance culture for a sustainable, profitable future.

Eight principles for enlisting and empowering others

1. **Demonstrate genuine care** – Show your team members that you care about them as whole individuals; about their well-being and their performance at home and at work. Create an environment where they feel inspired, encouraged and uplifted, knowing that their leader is truly invested in their success.

2. **Share a compelling vision** – Inspire your team by presenting a clear and exciting vision for the future. Help them understand how their efforts contribute to achieving this shared goal.

3. **Encourage courageous conversations and courageous actions** – Foster a culture where team members feel safe to engage in open, honest discussions and take calculated risks in pursuit of innovative solutions and improvements.

4. **Address their needs and concerns** – Be attuned to your team's challenges, opportunities and concerns. Provide the support and resources they need to overcome obstacles and achieve their objectives.

5. **Acknowledge and appreciate them often** – Recognise and appreciate your team members' thoughts, words and actions. Ensure they feel seen and heard, fostering a sense of belonging and value within the team. The more valued they feel, the more value they will add.

6. **Cultivate mutual trust** – Build trust by being both trusting of others and trustworthy. Show confidence in your team's abilities while demonstrating your own integrity and reliability.

7. **Create opportunities for meaningful contributions** – Empower your team members by providing opportunities for them to make a significant impact on projects and initiatives.

8. **Equip, enable and empower your people to figure it out along the way** – Clearly communicate the why behind what you want them to do, and then let them figure out the how. Give your team the freedom to explore and develop their own approaches to bringing that vision to life. Equip them with skills. Enable them with tools. Empower them to make decisions and let them pioneer the way forward. That will inspire a sense of ownership and engagement in the work they do.

In a coaching session with one of my clients, Laurent, we were talking about the importance of culture in a rapidly growing team. In order not to dilute a successful culture as new people join, he articulated it beautifully, saying, 'We need strong diffusers of culture.' What a brilliant analogy! I'm sure you can picture a diffuser, and potentially even imagine the scent of a diffuser filling the room. That's what you want for your business:

a positive culture that fills the room and engulfs anyone who walks into it.

With the right people on the right seats, doing the right things at the right time with the right DNA, you'll be able to take the bus wherever you want to go. You will also have confidence in their potential to become a high-performance team and achieve incredible things together.

Develop a high-performance team

In a fascinating *Harvard Business Review* article,[70] Alex 'Sandy' Pentland and his team of MIT's Human Dynamics Laboratory researchers set out on a mission to uncover the secret sauce behind high-performing teams. Hoping to decode the 'it factor' they asked a central question: 'Why do some teams consistently deliver high performance while other seemingly identical teams struggle?'

They engaged with a diverse range of teams from various projects and industries, equipping over 2,500 individuals with wearable electronic sensors that tracked their social interactions for weeks. The data revealed a striking pattern: the most crucial factor in a team's success was how they communicated. Communication patterns turned out to be as significant as all other factors combined, like intelligence, personality and talent. The researchers could even predict a team's success just by analysing their communication data, without ever laying eyes on the team members themselves.

What's the secret recipe for amazing team communication? Pentland identified three essential communication dynamics that impact performance:

1. **Energy** – How team members contribute to a team as a whole

2. **Engagement** – How team members communicate with one another

3. **Exploration** – How teams communicate with one another

By analysing the data, he was able to determine the perfect team patterns for each of these dynamics. Even better, he discovered that teams could significantly boost their performance by monitoring their communication patterns over time and adjusting to move closer to that ideal.

Dysfunctional vs high-performance teams

Having personally worked with individuals, teams and businesses across various industries in more than thirty-three countries around the world, I've seen the difference between good but slightly dysfunctional teams and great high-performance teams.

In organisations where the individuals and teams are not performing at their best, you're most likely to find good teams with high potential that are dysfunctional in the way they operate. Those teams will have talented, high-potential team members who feel like they are stagnating and are therefore potentially mentally checking out, if not physically resigning. You'll also find functional teams that are operating in silos, not collaborating or communicating effectively.

Dysfunctional teams are characterised by poor communication, lack of trust and unproductive conflict. They struggle to achieve their goals and often create a toxic work environment that hinders collaboration and overall performance.

Through our award-winning Liberating Greatness® high-performance coaching programmes, we help our clients bridge the gap from their current reality (described above) to their desire future reality (described below).

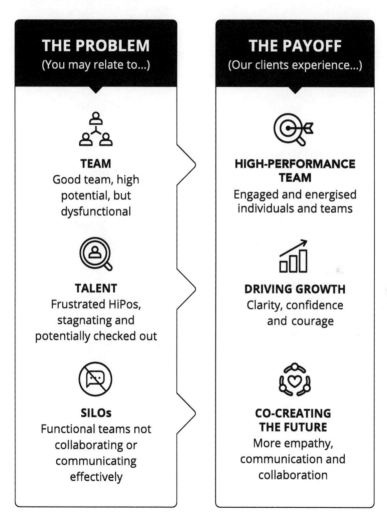

THE PROBLEM
(You may relate to...)

THE PAYOFF
(Our clients experience...)

TEAM
Good team, high potential, but dysfunctional

HIGH-PERFORMANCE TEAM
Engaged and energised individuals and teams

TALENT
Frustrated HiPos, stagnating and potentially checked out

DRIVING GROWTH
Clarity, confidence and courage

SILOs
Functional teams not collaborating or communicating effectively

CO-CREATING THE FUTURE
More empathy, communication and collaboration

High-performance teams are characterised by their ability to consistently deliver exceptional results while maintaining a positive and collaborative work environ-ment. These teams have highly engaged and energised individuals who drive growth with laser-focused clarity, confidence and courage, and as a result they communicate well, collaborate effectively and co-create the future.

The most effective, efficient, energised and engaged high-performance teams I've worked with consistently exhibit several key characteristics that contribute to their success:

- **Clear goals and objectives** – High-performance teams have a shared understanding of their goals and objectives, which helps align their efforts and maintain focus on achieving their desired outcomes.

- **Strong leadership** – Effective leaders inspire and motivate their team members, provide clear direction and foster an environment that supports teamwork, learning and growth.

- **Cognitive diversity** – High-performance teams are diverse and include people with a variety of skills, experiences and perspectives. They embrace the cognitive diversity that comes through different socio-economic backgrounds, frames of reference, generations, education, abilities, disabilities, gender, race, culture and ethnicities. This helps to bring a variety of ideas to the table and enables the team to be more innovative and adaptable.

- **Open communication** – High-performance teams prioritise open, honest and transparent communication. This allows for the free flow of ideas, constructive feedback and timely resolution of any issues or conflicts.

- **Trust and mutual respect** – Team members trust and respect one another, creating a strong foundation for collaboration, sharing of ideas and support in achieving their common goals.

- **A collaborative culture** – High-performance teams have a culture of collaboration, where members work together effectively towards a common goal, leveraging the unique strengths and skills of everyone to achieve the best possible results. This helps to create a sense of community and shared purpose.

- **Adaptability and flexibility** – These teams can adapt to changing circumstances and adjust their approach as needed to overcome challenges and capitalise on new opportunities.

- **Accountability and shared ownership** – Team members take responsibility for their actions and are held accountable for their results. This encourages ownership of tasks and fosters a sense of pride in their work.

- **High levels of engagement and commitment** – Members of high-performance teams are highly engaged in their work and display a strong commitment to achieving their goals.

- **A healthy balance between results and relationships** – High-performance teams maintain a healthy balance between focusing on results and nurturing positive relationships among team members. This balance ensures that team members feel valued and supported, while also driving them to achieve their goals.

- **Continuous learning and improvement** – High-performance teams have a commitment to learning, growth and continuous improvement. They regularly assess their performance, identify areas for development and implement strategies to enhance their skills and processes.

Cultivate these characteristics within your team and I guarantee that you will create an environment that promotes high performance, enhances overall productivity and ultimately contributes to the success and growth of the individuals, teams and organisation.

Develop, raise up and lead leaders

Your competitive advantage in the marketplace depends on your ability to raise up leaders faster than your competition. Not only am I talking about competition in your category, but I'm also talking about competition for the best talent in the world, across all categories. In today's post-pandemic world, the battle for top talent has become fiercer than ever. With remote work becoming the norm, you are no longer competing just within your category, industry or geography, but against the best talent across the globe, irrespective of location.

Simon Sinek, internationally recognised author, speaker and consultant who has transformed the way businesses think about leadership and impact, says in his book, *Find Your Why*, 'The greatest contribution of a leader, is to make other leaders.'[71]

In a world where access to top talent is increasingly competitive, your leadership skills play a crucial role in attracting, retaining and developing the best and the brightest. To stay ahead, you need to develop, raise up and lead leaders, providing them with the tools, resources and opportunities they need to excel in their roles.

When you add value to people by investing in their personal and professional development – leading, teaching, challenging and role modelling the way for them – you amplify your impact in the world. Create an environment that encourages leaders to develop themselves and their people.

Are you creating, nurturing and growing the leaders of tomorrow? Are you raising up leaders to seamlessly step into their next level? If not, now's your chance! If you want to significantly amplify your impact in the world, develop, raise up and lead leaders. Help them see beyond what you see and do more than what you've been able to do. Your legacy in business will be amplified to the next level through the leaders that you raise up to see more and achieve more that you ever could on your own.

Amplify your impact by managing well-designed systems and processes

Well-designed systems and processes are crucial for the smooth functioning of an organisation as they enable teams to operate more efficiently, reduce errors and improve overall performance. Effective systems also contribute to a clear understanding of roles and responsibilities, which promotes accountability and collaboration. By investing time and resources into developing robust systems and processes, leaders can create an environment that supports growth, innovation and long-term success.

Consider the findings presented in Michael E. Gerber's book, *The E-Myth Revisited*.[72] Gerber states that while 80% of small businesses fail, 75% of franchises succeed. The key difference? Franchises have well-established systems in place that ensure consistency, efficiency and scalability. One store serves a local community. Taking time to document systems and processes and train and develop people enables franchisors to expand with limitless potential. That one store in the local community has the potential to become multiple stores across multiple locations, nationally and internationally.

Take McDonald's as an example. The fast-food giant has meticulously crafted systems for everything, from food preparation and customer service to employee training and management, which has enabled the company to maintain its high standards across thousands of locations worldwide.

Another example of the power of systems can be found in the Entrepreneurial Operating System (EOS), a comprehensive business management framework designed to help entrepreneurs improve their companies' performance by implementing a set of proven processes, tools and disciplines.[73] By adopting the EOS, businesses can create a more structured and efficient environment, enabling them to better achieve their goals.

Apple's iOS is yet another testament to the importance of well-designed systems. The operating system's intuitive interface and consistent user experience across different devices have played a significant role in Apple's success. By maintaining a strong focus on system design, Apple has been able to deliver products that consistently delight their customers and stand out in a highly competitive market.

In each of these examples, the power of well-designed systems and processes is evident. By prioritising the development and implementation of effective systems, leaders can amplify their impact and set their organisations up for long-term success.

Often, when I'm working with clients, I find that the biggest thing holding them back is a lack of effective systems and processes. While my area of expertise leans towards sales and marketing systems, I've also worked with clients to identify improvements in their IT and project management systems to achieve both commercial and operational excellence. The result of systems-related projects is almost always clearer ways of working, aligned key performance indicators (KPIs), disciplined action and rigorous tracking, monitoring and measuring of progress.

Two of my mentors, twin brothers David and Jason Benham, who are entrepreneurs and co-authors of the book *Expert Ownership*,[74] encouraged me to become obsessed with systems. Their view is that systems run your business and people run your systems. Have poor systems and your people can only achieve so much. Great systems run by great people will enable you to build a successful business.

The Benham brothers have an acronym, SYSTEM, which stands for: 'Save yourself stress, time, effort, money.' Systems give you consistent results. The reason people find it easy to walk into a franchise store anywhere in the world is because they trust the brand that's built around standards and systems that are designed to create a predictable result. Systems will save you time and money and give you peace of mind to gain the results you expect and scale your operations – that's amplification.

Systematising for success

In your personal and professional lives, having robust systems and processes brings clarity, calm and composure to how you do what you do. If you want consistent results, look for areas of improvement, create and implement systems and processes, and continuously improve them as you run them. Follow these four steps to set up your systems.

Step 1: Identify areas for improvement

To amplify your impact through systems and processes, the first step is to identify areas in your personal or professional lives that require improvement. Assess your current systems by evaluating your daily routines, business operations and team interactions. Look for inefficiencies, bottlenecks or areas prone to errors. Seek feedback from team members, colleagues or family members to gain different perspectives on potential areas of improvement. By pinpointing these areas, you can prioritise which systems and processes to create or refine. To identify areas for improvement:

- **Track your time** – Tracking your time for a week or two will help you understand how you are allocating your resources, allowing you to spot inefficiencies, time-wasting activities or areas where you might need to streamline processes. By having a clear understanding of where your time is spent, you can make data-driven decisions to improve your systems.

- **Analyse your successes and challenges** – By understanding what has worked well in the past and where you have encountered difficulties, you can make informed decisions about which systems and processes to create or refine. This introspection can help you identify strengths to build upon and weaknesses to address, ensuring that your systems are optimised for success.

- **Benchmark against industry standards** – Comparing your current systems and processes with industry best practices or competitors can provide valuable insights into potential areas for improvement. By understanding what others are doing successfully, you can identify gaps in your own systems and processes that may be hindering your progress. This benchmarking exercise can help you set realistic goals for improvement and inform your decision-making as you create or refine systems to better align with industry standards and maintain a competitive edge.

This simple exercise helped my team identify areas for improvement in our customer success journey. Investing time, energy and resources in understanding where there were inefficiencies, where we dropped the ball in the past and what best practice should look like, enabled us to create better systems to enhance our customer experience.

Step 2: Create and implement systems

Once you have identified the areas that need attention, it's time to create and implement effective and efficient systems and processes. To do this:

- **Define clear objectives and desired outcomes** – Establish what you aim to achieve with your new or improved systems and processes. By setting clear goals, you can better direct your efforts and maintain focus throughout the development and implementation process.

- **Map out workflows** – Visualise each step involved in the system or process, from start to finish. Identify potential bottlenecks or areas of inefficiency and consider ways to streamline the workflow. Documenting these workflows can help ensure consistency and facilitate communication among team members.

- **Establish roles and responsibilities** – Clearly define the roles and responsibilities of everyone involved in the system or process. This clarity promotes accountability, collaboration and a sense of ownership among team members, ultimately leading to better results.

- **Set performance metrics** – Establish KPIs to measure the effectiveness of your systems and processes. Regularly track and review these metrics to assess whether the system is meeting its objectives and to identify areas for further improvement.

- **Create scorecards and dashboards** – Develop scorecards and dashboards to visually represent the performance metrics and KPIs of your systems and processes. These tools can help you easily monitor progress, identify trends and make data-driven decisions. By providing a clear, concise view of performance, scorecards and dashboards enable you and your team to stay aligned and focused on achieving the desired outcomes. What you measure and monitor improves.

- **Communicate and train** – Clearly communicate the new systems and processes to all relevant parties, ensuring they understand the purpose, benefits and their roles within the system. Provide any necessary training or resources to support their successful adoption. This may include written documentation, hands-on training sessions or ongoing coaching and support.

- **Monitor and adjust** – Continuously monitor the performance of your new or improved systems and processes, and make adjustments as needed. Regularly soliciting feedback from team members or stakeholders can help you identify areas where further improvements can be made, ensuring your systems remain effective and efficient over time.

Step 3: Continuous improvement

Embrace a mindset of continuous improvement to ensure that your systems and processes evolve and adapt as needed. Regularly review the effectiveness of your systems, considering any changes in your business environment or personal circumstances. Learn from both your successes and failures and use this knowledge to refine your systems and processes.

Encourage open communication and feedback from those involved, fostering a culture where improvements are seen as opportunities rather than criticisms.

The Japanese principle of 'Kaizen', which means 'change for the better' or 'continuous improvement', is a business philosophy that emphasises the importance of making small, incremental improvements in processes and systems over time. By incorporating the Kaizen mindset into your approach to continuous improvement, you can create a culture of learning and growth, where all members of your organisation are encouraged to identify opportunities for improvement and work together to refine your systems and processes. This can lead to increased efficiency, effectiveness and overall success. We spoke about marginal gains earlier in the book, recognising that small changes consistently over time compound to achieve significant shifts.

Celebrate opportunities to make improvements on your quest for excellence – the gradual result of always striving to be better.

Step 4: Balance flexibility and structure

While having structured systems and processes in place is crucial for efficiency and effectiveness, it's equally important to strike a balance with flexibility and adaptability. Recognise that unforeseen circumstances or changes may arise and be prepared to adjust your systems and processes accordingly. Empower your team or family members to make informed decisions within the boundaries of the established systems, allowing for creativity and innovation. By finding the right balance between flexibility and structure, you can maintain efficiency while remaining agile and responsive to changing needs.

In fostering an environment of flexibility and adaptability, it's important to create a culture that values open communication, collaboration and continuous learning. Encourage team or family members to share their ideas, experiences and insights, and be open to incorporating their suggestions into your systems and processes. Involving those who are directly affected by the systems creates a more inclusive and adaptable framework that addresses the needs of everyone involved. Regularly revisit your systems and processes to ensure they remain relevant and responsive to changing circumstances, and don't be afraid to adjust when necessary. Strike the right balance between structure and flexibility and you'll create a dynamic and resilient environment that encourages growth and innovation.

By incorporating these strategies into your approach to systems and processes, you can amplify your impact and set yourself, your team and your organisation up for long-term success.

Amplify your impact by using your influence

As you amplify your impact by leading people and managing systems, you'll create opportunities for greater influence. Your actions and decisions carry significant weight, and by harnessing this influence you can foster a culture of growth, innovation and excellence within your organisation or personal network.

Influence will mean different things to different people. Your frame of reference may come from role models who've positively impacted your life by teaching you how to think and behave, challenging you to be better because they could see your potential to be, do and have more, and living their lives by example. You may have also had people in your life and career that have demonstrated how *not* to think and behave, negatively influencing you and others around them.

For me, influence always comes down to intention. If your intention is to inspire, encourage, uplift and make a positive impact in the lives of those you're leading, that's positive influence. If your intention is for your own gain, potentially at the cost of others, that's manipulation.

Desmond Tutu, the South African Anglican bishop and social rights activist recognised the power of influence and its role in promoting positive change. One of his famous quotes is, 'Do your little bit of good where you are; it's those little bits of good put together that overwhelm the world.'[75]

He indeed overwhelmed the world with his joy, faith, love and compassion, and his message of peace, forgiveness and reconciliation. Each person can have a positive impact on the world through their actions, no matter how small they may seem. You have the power to influence your surroundings and contribute to a larger collective effort to create a better world.

When I think of the impact I want to have in the world, I think about how I can use my time, my talent and my treasure. That's what I have control over; everything I have at my disposal to give. There is such a great need in the world that solving all its problems seems overwhelming. Like Tutu, Saint Francis of Assisi said, 'All the darkness in the world cannot extinguish the light of a single candle.'[76]

That's what I want to be, and what I want to encourage you to be; a single candle in the world, shining light for others to see and inspiring them to let their light shine too.

How will you give your time, talent and treasure to amplify your impact?

By focusing on these three areas, you can effectively amplify your impact and use your influence for the greater good:

- **Time:** Time is one of our most precious resources. By consciously choosing where and how you invest your time, you can create a lasting impact on the lives of those around you. Whether it's mentoring others, volunteering in your community or simply being present for those who need your support, your time can make a significant difference.

- **Talent:** Each of us possesses unique skills, knowledge and abilities that can be used to positively influence others. By sharing your expertise, you can help others grow, develop and overcome challenges. Be generous with your knowledge and use your talents to uplift and empower those around you. This could involve teaching, coaching or simply being a resource for others as they navigate their own journey.

- **Treasure:** Your financial resources, possessions, contacts, strategic partnerships and other assets can also be used to make a positive impact. Consider how you can use your resources to support worthy causes, invest in people and organisations that align with your values or help individuals in need. By sharing your treasure, you can create opportunities for others and contribute to a more equitable and just world.

Using your influence with intention and focusing on your time, talent and treasure can create a ripple effect, inspiring others to follow suit and take similar actions. As more individuals recognise their own potential for influence and use it for the greater good, this collective effort can lead to significant change and improvement in the world around us.

You can be that pebble in the water that positively disrupts the status quo and creates a ripple effect. Your influence is not solely about the position you hold or the resources at your disposal; it's about the way you choose to live your life and the impact you have on others. Lead by example, demonstrate kindness and empathy, and always strive to leave a positive imprint on the lives of those you encounter. By doing so, you will not only amplify your impact but also inspire others to do the same, within your organisation, personal network and beyond.

What do you want to amplify?

What impact and influence would you like to have in the world? Maybe it's a positive, significant impact on one of the global goals for sustainable development? Or perhaps it's making a positive, significant impact in your children's lives, or on the lives of your family, friends, loved ones, community or team? It'll be different for each of us, and it's not for me to say what you should amplify. That's for you to decide.

My challenge to you... decide! Commit to your decision and take positive action to following through.

Summary

Take a moment to reflect on the immense potential you hold to create meaningful change in the world. Embrace the idea that by amplifying your efforts, you can have a more significant impact on the lives of those around you and the causes that matter most to you. Remember that effective leadership, efficient systems and using your influence are essential tools in your quest to liberate your greatness.

By harnessing the power of amplification, you can not only elevate your own achievements but also inspire and empower others to reach their full potential, creating a world where greatness thrives. Lead people, manage systems and use your influence to amplify your impact – that's the Principle of Amplification.

Practical application

Reflect on the Principle of Amplification

Reflection is a skill. Take a moment to capture your thoughts and commit to taking consistent action to move the needle forward.

- What key insights did you discover in this chapter?

- What decisions are you committed to making to gain the greatest return?

- What disciplined action will you take in the next week/month/quarter that will give you the greatest reward?

Activity

In the spirit of striving for excellence and continual improvement, what will you...

STOP
(Doing / thinking
/ believing / feeling)

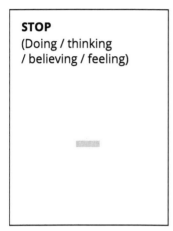

START
(Doing / thinking
/ believing / feeling)

CONTINUE
(Doing / thinking
/ believing / feeling)

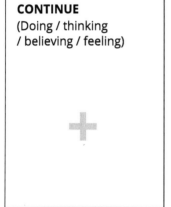

LEARN
(Book / online course
/ audio)

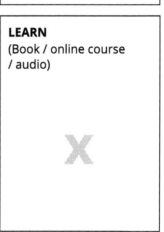

Additional resources

For bonus videos and downloadable content related to the Principle of Amplification, visit: www.liberateyourgreatness. com/amplification.

EIGHT

The Principle Of Acceleration

Innovate, communicate, collaborate and co-create to accelerate from 0 to 1 to 100

On the journey to liberating your greatness, embracing the Principle of Acceleration is essential for rapid progress and growth. Especially in today's fast-paced world, the ability to adapt, innovate and accelerate is crucial for business leaders and entrepreneurs.

This chapter will provide you with the necessary strategies, tools and techniques to help you move forward quickly and effectively, ensuring that you stay ahead of the competition and continuously grow in your personal and professional lives. We will explore concepts such as design thinking, innovation theory and the 0–1–100 framework, which can help you navigate challenges, optimise your strategies and accelerate your success.

We'll also talk through key growth accelerators that will significantly drive your life and business forward.

By adopting an agile mindset and being open to continuous learning and improvement, you will be better equipped to reach your goals with greater speed and efficiency.

Amplify before you accelerate. If you accelerate before you amplify, you'll miss out on the opportunity for even greater impact. When you have a small flywheel spinning fast, you will have some degree of positive impact, but it won't be as significant as when you amplify it first. Once you've applied the Principle of Amplification, the Principle of Acceleration will help you to achieve phenomenal results.

An era of accelerating change

The concept of accelerating change is a philosophy championed by visionaries like Ray Kurzweil, Hans Moravec and Vernor Vinge. They argue that a singularity will occur as a result of the self-reinforcing nature of technological advancements. 'Technological singularity' is often used to describe a hypothetical future point in time when technological growth becomes uncontrollable and irreversible, resulting in unforeseeable changes to human civilisation. Today, the pace of change is significantly faster than it was during any other period in history. The accelerating change thesis predicts that future change will be even more rapid than it is today.

Undeniably, we are living in an era of rapid and accelerating change. In recent years, we have witnessed dramatic shifts on a global scale that have reshaped our world in unprecedented ways. Political upheavals have reverberated across the United States, South America, Europe and Asia, stirring tensions and reshaping power dynamics.

Brexit marked a significant turning point, as the United Kingdom's departure from the European Union altered the political and economic landscape of Europe, with far-reaching implications for trade, immigration and international relations.

The COVID-19 pandemic brought about sweeping changes and challenges, enforcing lockdowns world-wide and causing economic turmoil. It has disrupted our traditional ways of living and working, leading not only to a physical health crisis but also inciting wide-spread mental health and financial crises.

The Russian invasion of Ukraine ignited the largest-scale land war in Europe since the Balkan wars of the 1990s – a stark reminder of the fragile state of global peace.

Economic instability has led to inflation, recession and even the collapse of at least three small- to mid-size US banks that failed because of significant exposures to cryptocurrencies, which rose to dizzy heights and have since crashed.

The environmental changes we are experiencing are also significant, marking an urgent call for sustainability and conservation efforts. On top of these, we are grappling with widespread human rights injustices across various regions.

In short, the world as we knew it has been drastically reshaped by these sweeping changes, emphasising the necessity for adaptability and resilience in our rapidly evolving landscape.

With danger comes opportunity

Despite the news, not all is doom and gloom. The Chinese word for crisis has two meanings: 'danger' and 'opportunity'. While the danger is often unavoidable, the opportunity, on the other hand, depends on how we react to the danger. Every crisis, every change environment, every next level always brings with it both danger and opportunity.

High-performing leaders consider both potential realities. They assess the situation pessimistically to understand worst-case scenarios and acknowledge and mitigate the risks. They also assess the situation optimistically to create best-case scenarios, looking for the opportunities to lead people through the storm, navigate the challenges, overcome obstacles and succeed against all odds. Considering both sides, they decide to move forward then act courageously, despite fear.

In the face of global shifts, there has been a surge of innovation, new ways of thinking and behaving. We've seen an acceleration in digital transformation across businesses of all sizes as companies have had to adapt to remote work and online commerce. AI has changed the game in so many industries already, bringing with it much controversy over the benefits and dangers. The healthcare industry has made significant strides in vaccine research and deployment, demonstrating its capacity for rapid adaptation and innovation.

Furthermore, the environmental crisis has sparked a wave of sustainability-focused initiatives, from renewable energy to zero-waste practices. Governments, corporations and individuals alike are increasingly recognising the importance of sustainable living and are taking steps to reduce their environmental impact. The B-Corp movement is gaining momentum as businesses acknowledge the benefits of making consistent, marginal gains on their sustainability scorecards.

On a societal level, important issues like racial injustice and gender inequality are being more openly discussed and confronted. Movements for social justice are gaining momentum, pushing for systemic changes and greater equality. That's also highlighted the need for more diversity, equity, inclusion and belonging initiatives, not just for policy's sake, but to embrace cognitive diversity for greater thought partnerships.

In times of crisis, our response to change can generally be categorised into three types:

1. **Fight** – This response is characterised by confronting the change or crisis head-on. Those who adopt this approach often exhibit resilience, courage and determination. They are not afraid to face adversity and are ready to tackle the challenges that come with change. They take control of their thoughts, words and actions, upskill, add value in the world, derive greater value and move the needle forward. They actively seek solutions, make necessary adjustments and persist in their efforts to overcome obstacles.

2. **Flight** – This response is marked by evasion or withdrawal. When faced with change or crisis, some individuals may choose to retreat or avoid the situation altogether. This could be due to fear, anxiety or a feeling of overwhelm. It's important to remember that while this may provide temporary relief, the underlying issues remain and will need to be addressed eventually.

3. **Freeze** – This response involves becoming immobilised in the face of change or crisis. It can be likened to a deer caught in the headlights, unsure of which direction to take. This state of inaction is often a result of shock, confusion or a sense of helplessness. In such cases, seeking support, guidance and reassurance can be crucial

in helping individuals unfreeze and start taking proactive steps.

Reflecting on our Liberating Greatness Framework, where all proactive change starts with awareness, what do you tend to do in crisis situations? Do you fight, take flight or freeze? Gaining awareness of your instinctive reactions to change is the first step towards navigating crisis situations with grace and resilience. It allows you to understand your default patterns and make conscious decisions about how you want to respond. Remember, every crisis presents an opportunity for growth and learning. Embrace change as an integral part of your journey towards personal and professional greatness. It is through these experiences that you will discover your inner strength, resilience and capacity to thrive in the face of adversity.

So, while this era of accelerating change brings with it immense challenges, it also presents opportunities for growth, innovation and progress. As a leader, what are you doing to personally keep up with change, recognise the opportunities and inspire proactive change in your organisation? Are you demonstrating the mental agility to pivot quickly and be a catalyst for positive transformation? Your people need you to be strong and courageous, lead them through the storm, and help them accept and embrace change.

Four keys to accepting and embracing change

There are two types of change: change that happens to you and change that you make happen.

The former is inevitable, uncontrolled, often surprising and can sometimes be overwhelming. It is a testament to the dynamic nature of life and the world we live in, as described above.

The latter, however, is within your control. It is the active manifestation of your choices, decisions and actions. This type of change is powerful, for it is borne from your own will and initiative. When you choose to make change happen, you are asserting your agency, shaping your destiny and actively participating in the narrative of your life and business. You are transforming from a passive recipient of change or even a victim of change to an active driver of it, empowered to steer your life, your team, and your business towards a brighter future.

When I work with high-performing teams in various organisations, industries and markets, I encourage them to apply the following four keys to proactively accepting and embracing change to accelerate their growth.

Key 1: Innovate to accelerate

Innovation is not just about coming up with new ideas, it's about turning those ideas into reality in a way that adds value. It's a critical component of long-term success and acceleration. Organisations that innovate gain a competitive advantage by finding new and better ways to serve their clients. They optimise their systems and processes to become more efficient and productive. They discover more sustainable practices, products and services, while building internal adaptability and resilience. Ultimately, they accelerate their growth and success.

Create a culture of innovation

Encourage risk-taking and creative thinking within your team or organisation. Arla Foods – the Danish cooperative and one of the largest producers of dairy products in Europe – is a shining example of a culture of innovation. Recognising the ever-evolving needs of their consumers and the increasing demands of sustainable production, Arla Foods is deeply committed to innovative solutions, as reflected in their vision for 'Creating the future of dairy to bring health and inspiration to the world, naturally.'[77]

One of the best years in my corporate career was working at Arla Foods in Denmark, where I developed their global sales academy and had the privilege of working with amazing people, participating in and leading innovation workshops. The Arla Innovation Centre is best in class, and their culture of innovation is inspiring and aspirational.

Arla Foods has created an environment where innovative thinking is encouraged and rewarded. Their employees are empowered to experiment and take risks, knowing that failure is viewed as a stepping stone to success rather than a deterrent. You'll find pockets of innovation taking place throughout the organisation. This culture of innovation has allowed Arla Foods to stay at the forefront of the dairy industry, continually introducing new products and improving existing ones to meet their customers' changing tastes and dietary needs.

Arla Foods applies innovation not just to their products but also to their processes. They continually seek ways to optimise their operations, reducing waste and increasing efficiency. Through innovative technology and machinery, they have managed to streamline their production process, resulting in cost savings and a reduced environmental footprint.

One of their most significant innovations is their commitment to sustainability. Recognising the impact of dairy farming on the environment, Arla Foods has set ambitious goals to reduce their carbon emissions and water usage. Through innovative farming practices and the use of renewable energy, they are making substantial strides towards achieving these goals.

Innovation in Arla Foods is not just a buzzword or a 'nice to have' – it's an integral part of their strategy for growth and success. Their culture of innovation has allowed them to remain competitive, respond swiftly to market changes and continue delivering high-quality products that their customers love. Through their example, we can see how innovation accelerates progress and paves the way for a better future.

Go from concept to rollout in 0–1–100

The 0–1–100 innovation principle is a powerful approach to bringing new ideas and products to market. By breaking down the process into three distinct stages, you can minimise risk, maximise learning and accelerate the path to success. Here's how I bring the 0–1–100 innovation principle to life with clients.

Concept (0): The first stage involves brainstorming and conceptualising your idea. At this point, you're identifying the problem you want to solve or the opportunity you want to seize. Consider the needs, concerns, challenges and opportunities of your target audience, the feasibility of your solution and its potential impact. Conduct market research, gather feedback and refine your concept until you have a solid foundation.

One of my favourite four-day innovation sprints that I've facilitated was for Tesco, the UK's largest retailer, to create a new offering for one of their categories. We spent the first two days seeking to understand the category, shoppers and consumers' needs, challenges, concerns and opportunities, then explored design principles and best practices before ideating potential solutions. The time invested up front was well worth it, as the team began ideating on the back of the insights they had gained in the first two days.

During this phase of your innovation process, think divergently and convergently, capturing ideas without judgement initially. Divergent thinking is the process of generating many different ideas about a topic in a spontaneous, free-flowing manner. It's often associated with creativity and 'thinking outside the box'. Divergent thinking encourages going in many different directions to generate a variety of possible solutions. Brainstorming is a common example of divergent thinking, where the goal is to come up with as many ideas as possible, without worrying about feasibility or practicality at this stage. Convergent thinking, on the other hand, is the process of narrowing down multiple ideas into a single solution. It involves analysing, evaluating and critiquing the ideas that have been generated through divergent thinking. This process encourages logical thinking, decision-making and prioritisation to arrive at the best or most feasible solution.

In an effective problem-solving process, both divergent and convergent thinking are necessary. You start with divergent thinking to explore all possible solutions, then switch to convergent thinking to evaluate the ideas and decide on the best course of action. This combination allows for creativity and innovation, while maintaining a practical focus on achieving the desired outcome.

As Einstein once said, 'We cannot solve our problems with the same thinking we used when we created them.'[78] He also said, 'Insanity is doing the same thing over and over again and expecting different results.'[79] To get different results, to inspire game-changing new ideas and breakthrough initiatives, you must think differently and do different things.

Pilot or prototype (1): The next stage involves creating a pilot or prototype of your idea. This initial version serves as a proof of concept, allowing you to test your idea in a controlled environment before committing significant resources to a full-scale rollout. Use this stage to gather data, identify potential challenges and refine your solution based on real-world feedback.

Test, learn and iterate. Experiment with new ideas, analyse the results, learn from the outcomes and refine your strategies accordingly. Create a strong desire for continual improvement; an obsessive drive to be better and to achieve more.

This iterative process enables rapid progress and continuous improvement. It's essential to be open to iteration and improvement during this phase, as it lays the groundwork for the final stage. Ultimately what you're looking for is successful proof of concept. My team and I often start with pilot programmes for our clients to show proof of concept before cascading through the entire organisation. It's a highly effective and efficient way of onboarding new teams, minimising risk for the client and maximising their ROI.

Full rollout (100): Once you've tested, learnt and iterated on your pilot or prototype, it's time to move into full-scale rollout. At this point, you have a refined solution that has been validated by real-world experience, making it far more likely to succeed. During the rollout, monitor the performance of your solution, gather additional feedback and make any necessary adjustments to ensure its ongoing success.

The 0–1–100 innovation principle not only helps you bring your ideas to life but also ensures that you do so in a way that maximises their potential for success. By adopting this approach, you can accelerate your growth, stay ahead of the competition and drive meaningful impact in your industry.

Learn faster to grow faster

The quicker you learn while implementing a 0–1–100 approach to innovation, the quicker you'll grow, both personally and professionally. Steve Brass, CEO of WD-40 Company, inspires individuals and teams at WD-40 Company to learn faster to grow faster, creating a sense of urgency to stay ahead of the competition and the frenetic pace of change in the world.

In an interview with Steve, I asked him what he does to ensure he's continually learning and growing as a role model for his people to follow. He responded by expressing his passion for continuous improvement and learning, looking externally and internally for new and better ways of thinking and behaving. He believes that learning is exciting and he taps into resources like *HBR* articles, Google and best practices from around the world. He remains open and curious and asks questions to learn daily. Within his first 100 days as CEO, Steve embarked on a listening tour to ask questions, listen to his people across all the trading blocs and learn from them, before creating his strategic drivers for the future. WD-40 has innovation in its DNA, and Steve has set the tone for acceleration because of his desire for everyone in the business to learn faster to grow faster.

Leaders like Steve are lifelong learners. I'm sure you can resonate with your own passion for learning and development. You know that to do things that you've never done, you must learn what you don't yet know. You recognise the importance of staying informed about the latest trends, technologies and best practices in your industry to fuel innovation and accelerate growth. The fastest way you do that is to learn from someone who's already figured it out. Articles, books, courses, seminars, workshops, mentors and coaches will help you accelerate your learning.

There are several different learning style models that have been proposed, but one of the most well known is the VARK[80] model, developed by Neil Fleming, a New Zealand teacher and educational theorist. This model identifies four main learning styles: visual, auditory, reading/writing and kinaesthetic:

- **Visual** – Visual learners prefer to use images, maps and graphic organisers to understand information and ideas. They often visualise information and experiences in their minds.

- **Auditory** – Auditory learners prefer to hear information rather than reading it or seeing it displayed visually. They may prefer lectures, discussions and audio recordings as learning methods.

- **Read/write** – Read/write learners prefer to learn information through reading and writing tasks. They enjoy reading books and taking notes, and they often express a strong preference for text-based input and output.

- **Kinaesthetic** – Kinaesthetic learners prefer to learn through experience and movement. They learn best by doing or through physical interaction with the learning material.

What's your preferred learning style? How do your team members like to learn? How might you harness each person's learning style to accelerate their growth?

If you want to grow faster, you must learn faster. If you want to learn faster, learn with purpose and be professionally curious. One of the fastest ways to create a culture of learning is to encourage curiosity. Enable people with the tools and time to experiment, make mistakes, learn from them and share the lessons learnt.

Fail fast, fail often, fail forward

You might find it strange that I'm talking about failing in a chapter about acceleration. The truth is, failing is one of the quickest ways to learn and grow. Fear of failure is also one of the main reasons individuals, teams and businesses don't grow as fast as they should.

When I was at university in Cape Town, South Africa, I remember driving my maroon Citi Golf along the base of Table Mountain, listening to Tony Robbins talking about definitions of success and failure. While I had clarity on what success might look like for me at that stage in my life and my future, he challenged me to think differently about my definition of failure. When I reframed failure in terms of defining moments for me to learn and grow, an entire universe of opportunity opened up in front of me.

My personal definition of failure: If I 'fail' at something but learn one thing that can help me or someone else in future, then I'm succeeding. As long as I'm failing forward, I'm succeeding!

From that moment on, I believed that anything was possible (and I've kept failing forward ever since). I'm OK to fail, provided I'm learning, so I strive for progress over perfection. I aim for continual improvement; to get 1% better on every iteration. You may have heard the phrase, 'FAIL = first attempt in learning'? So true!

In his pursuit of inventing the light bulb, Thomas Edison famously said, 'I have not failed. I've just found 10,000 ways that won't work.'[81] That reflects Edison's determination and persistence in his work. Instead of being discouraged by the numerous attempts that did not result in a successful invention, he viewed each failure as a step closer to finding the solution. Embracing failure is a necessary part of the learning process and a means of achieving success.

If AI were to learn a new game, it would make a move and learn from the outcome of the action. If the move resulted in a successful outcome, it will celebrate it and remember that it worked. If the move resulted in an unsuccessful outcome, it will celebrate it and remember that it didn't work. When AI fails it doesn't judge itself, it just collects data points. It celebrates both outcomes, all because it's collecting data points on what works and what doesn't. That's how it's accelerating its own learning (with, of course, all the clever tech driving it).

One of my favourite business podcasts is *The Diary of a CEO with Steven Bartlett*. As discussed previously, at the end of each episode Steven asks his guest to write down a question to ask his next guest. At the end of episode 161, Brian Armstrong, founder of Coinbase, suggested the following question: 'What is the crazy big idea you would try if you could not fail?'[82] What a great question.

Here are some alternative meanings for the acronym 'FAIL' that deliver the same optimistic essence of the belief that you could not fail, or my view on failing forward:

- Finding another inspiring lesson
- Forward action inspires learning
- Frequently adjusting and improving life
- Faithful and intentional learning
- Forever advancing in learning

Which is your favourite? Pick one and fall in love with the process of failing forward. How do you define failure?

The path to success is often dotted with failures. Ask any successful person and they'll likely share stories of setbacks and stumbles along their journey. It's these failures that act as stepping stones, driving them to innovate, to find better ways of doing things and to become more persuasive in convincing others to support their dreams.

Consider Michael Jordan, one of the greatest basketball players of all time, who once said, 'I have failed over and over and over again in my life, and that is why I succeed.'[83] His failures on and off the court didn't deter him; instead, they fuelled his determination to succeed.

Then there's J.K. Rowling, the renowned author of the *Harry Potter* series. Her manuscript was rejected twelve times before finally being published. She didn't let those rejections stop her; instead, she persevered, believing in her work and its potential, as she explained in her Harvard University commencement speech.[84]

Let's not forget Walt Disney, a man whose vision transformed entertainment. Before his dreams became a reality, Disney was rejected by numerous banks over 300 times![85] He didn't let those rejections deter him. Instead, he remained steadfast in his pursuit, turning his dream into an iconic brand.

The key message from all these stories is clear: You can't let failure define you; you must let failures teach and guide you. Let them show you what to do differently next time because failure is not the opposite of success, it's part of it.

In the spirit of failing forward, I believe that yesterday's success is today's mediocrity and tomorrow's failure. Let's embrace failing forward through continuous improvement, adaptation and not resting on past achievements. What might you achieve if you commit to failing fast, failing more often and failing forward?

Innovate beyond products

Often when we think of innovation, we think of product and technology innovation. You can apply the principles of innovation to so many different areas of your business, though.

Created by Doblin Consulting (now known as Deloitte Digital), the Ten Types of Innovation® framework provides a way to identify new opportunities beyond products and develop viable innovations.[86] As stated by Keeley *et al* in the book *Ten Types of Innovation*, 'Successful innovators analyse the patterns of innovation in their industry. They make conscious, considered choices to innovate in different ways.'[87]

I recently spent a day with two senior leaders of a large multinational organisation to innovate the structure of their leadership team. The goal was to create a future-focused structure that would ensure the successful delivery of their seven-year strategy and growth targets. Understanding what the business requirements and needs of all relevant stakeholders were and then working through a process of ideating and iterating enabled us to create a brilliant new organisational design that will enable the people and business to thrive well beyond the initial target dates.

The same applies to many of the entrepreneurs I work with. Especially when industries are disrupted and operating models become less lucrative, entrepreneurs need to pivot, quickly. I've had so many inspiring conversations with clients that start stressfully because of changing economic conditions and end with genius ideas to unlock new revenue streams, reach new clients and make a positive impact in the world. That's the power of innovation.

Key 2: Communicate to accelerate

Every successful leader knows that you need to be able to communicate effectively if you want to positively influence people to make positive changes. Great leaders also know that you must move people mentally and emotionally if you want to make significant shifts. As Maya Angelou famously said, 'I've learned that people will forget what you said, people will forget what you did, but people will never forget how you made them feel.'[88]

There are hundreds of books and courses available to help you become a better communicator. Rather than focusing on how to communicate, I'm going to concentrate on how you want people to feel if you want to communicate to accelerate.

There are four desired outcomes of your communication:

1. **Connection** – Help people connect themselves to your story, your message and the goal you're striving to achieve or the cause you're fighting for. Help them connect with each other and with the purpose, mission, vision, values and goals of the organisation. Connection comes first, then comes direction.

2. **Clarity** – When you've established connection, give your people direction. Tell them what they need to know so that they feel that they have clarity and purposeful direction on the action plan, roles, responsibilities, desired outcomes and timelines. Clarity brings peace, focus and attention.

3. **Confidence** – Inspire people to feel confident in the plan and the finer details, and more importantly, to feel confident in you and your team's ability to execute the plan excellently.

4. **Courage** – When people feel connected, clear on the course of action and confident in the plan and the people, they are more likely to take courageous action.

Why is important for people to feel a sense of connection, clarity, confidence and courage? Well, quite simply, if they don't you won't move them to think or behave differently. If nothing changes, nothing changes.

One of the biggest challenges I see in organisations where functional teams are operating in silos or team members lack clarity and purposeful direction, or feel disconnected from their leaders, is due to poor communication. The good news is that this gap can be bridged with deliberate effort and intention. Improving your communication skills is one of the most powerful ways you can accelerate positive change, within both your team and your broader organisation.

Communication is the conduit through which information, inspiration and influence flow. If this conduit is blocked, distorted or even just inefficient, it can have a profound impact on your team's morale, productivity and potential for innovation. Conversely, when communication flows smoothly and effectively, it can galvanise a team, sparking creativity, enhancing collaboration and driving ambitious outcomes.

Connection, clarity, confidence and courage are the four cornerstones of effective communication because they address both the cognitive and emotional dimensions of human experience. They ensure that people not only understand what they need to do but also why they should do it, how they can do it, and what it means for them and for others. This creates a powerful alignment between action, purpose and values – a true catalyst for positive change.

Take a moment to reflect on your own communication practices. Are you creating connection, promoting clarity, boosting confidence and encouraging courage? If not, where can you make improvements? Remember, communication is not a one-size-fits-all solution. Different people and situations call for different communication strategies. Be adaptable, be responsive and above all, be authentic. The impact on your ability to accelerate positive change will be significant.

Follow these practical tips to achieve the four desired outcomes of your communication:

- **Create connection** – Connection is established through empathy, understanding and shared experiences. Show authenticity in your communication, allow vulnerability and listen actively to understand and relate to the concerns, ideas and feelings of others. Your ability to create a genuine connection will foster a sense of inclusion, belonging, trust and loyalty.

- **Promote clarity** – Clear communication is as much about seeking clarity as it is about giving clarity. Clarity comes from precision, simplicity and consistency in communication. Avoid jargon, be specific and provide context to ensure that your messages are easily understood. Reinforce key points and ensure that your audience has a clear understanding of the next steps.

- **Boost confidence** – Confidence is built through assurance, competence and reliability. Display your expertise and commitment, recognise and address concerns and provide clear evidence of past successes. Consistently deliver on your promises and be transparent about challenges, showing how they will be handled.

- **Encourage courage** – Courage is inspired by confidence but also by creating a safe space for risk-taking. Celebrate innovative thinking, even when it doesn't lead to success. Acknowledge the courage it takes to voice differing opinions, take on challenging tasks or admit mistakes. Show your own courage as a leader, demonstrating that you too are willing to step outside of your comfort zone for the sake of progress.

Remember, communication is not only about the message but also about how it's delivered. Pay attention to your tone of voice, body language and choice of words. Use various methods of communication – verbal, written and visual – to appeal to different learning styles. Choose the most effective medium for your message and the audience. Finally, ensure there is a feedback loop in your communication process. Encourage questions, comments and ideas, fostering a culture of open dialogue and mutual respect.

Key 3: Collaborate to accelerate

Teams that play well together, accelerate growth together. Teams don't always play well together, though. I've seen high-performing teams achieve fantastic results, consistently over twelve to twenty-four months, while making a positive impact on the individuals and business, until they make changes. We know that change is important for growth and that it comes with growing pains. With promotions, new structures and new team dynamics, what was once a highly functioning, successful team could spin into disarray. Why?

The Tuckman stages of team development,[89] proposed by psychologist Bruce Tuckman in 1965, is a widely recognised model that describes the progression of a team's dynamics across four stages:

1. Forming

2. Storming

3. Norming

4. Performing

This framework provides a roadmap for understanding how teams evolve, manage conflict, establish norms and ultimately work efficiently towards their goals. It's an invaluable tool for leaders seeking to navigate the complexities of team development and enhance group performance.

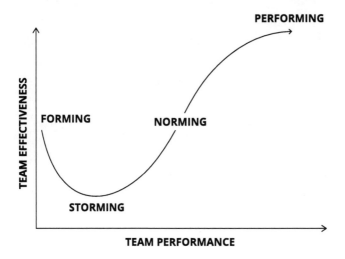

Often teams form with great intentions to collaborate, recognising the opportunity for synergy, potentially because of a mandate to do so. When the individuals start to butt heads a little, storming takes place and that's often where collaboration ends. Where, in fact, teams need to be able to work through storming by collaborating even more, seeking to understand each other other's perspectives and making a concerted effort to find common ground. When they do so, they're able to move on to norming and then performing.

Great leaders inspire and facilitate great collaborations. They intuitively know that great collaborations will accelerate the path to high performance. They understand that the beauty of collaboration is not just in combining efforts but in the fusion of diverse perspectives, talents and experiences that can foster innovation, drive efficiency and achieve common goals more effectively.

While collaboration may seem straightforward, it requires careful nurturing. Leaders need to create an environment where trust and open communication thrive. This involves acknowledging and appreciating individual contributions, encouraging constructive feedback and promoting a sense of shared responsibility. It's about making each team member feel valued and understood.

Successful collaborations are developed through a continuous process of learning, adjusting and growing together as a team. That requires patience and resilience, as people get to know each other and find effective ways of working together and solving problems. Leaders need to help the team navigate these challenges by emphasising the shared vision and values that bind the team together.

In the end, when a team effectively collaborates, they not only overcome obstacles and meet their goals but they also build a stronger, more cohesive unit. This is why collaboration is so powerful in accelerating growth:

- **Synergistic relationships** – Building synergistic relationships can help to pool the strengths of individuals, accelerating the achievement of shared goals. Those who excel at collaboration understand the simple but powerful truth: together they can achieve far more than they ever could alone.

- **Diverse teams** – Diversity in teams brings a wealth of experiences, ideas and skills to the table. This can turbocharge creativity and problem solving. Embracing cognitive diversity, or the inclusion of different ways of thinking and processing information, is particularly crucial.

- **Shared goals** – A shared understanding of goals and objectives aligns everyone's efforts, ensuring everyone is pulling in the same direction, thereby accelerating progress.

- **Shared challenges and opportunities** – When challenges and opportunities are shared, they become less daunting and more manageable. This collective approach can spark innovative solutions and strategies, speeding up growth and development.

- **Shared solutions** – Collaborative problem solving not only speeds up the solution-finding process but also ensures that the solutions are more robust, having been scrutinised and refined by diverse perspectives.

- **Team empowerment** – Empowering your team members to make decisions can streamline operations and foster a sense of ownership. This empowerment can lead to quicker decision-making and a more agile, responsive team.

- **Collaborative tools** – Leveraging collaborative tools and technologies can facilitate communication and coordination among team members. This is particularly essential in today's world of remote or hybrid working environments, where digital collaboration tools can bridge distances and time zones.

Collaboration is not just a 'nice to have', it's a necessity for accelerating growth and achieving sustainable success. Whether it's within your team or through strategic partnerships, collaboration combines a diversity of talents, experiences and perspectives that fuel creativity, drive innovation and enhance problem solving. It creates a synergy where the whole becomes greater than the sum of its parts.

Remember, collaboration is more than working together; it's about working together effectively. It requires mutual respect, open communication, shared goals and a collective commitment to success. As leaders, fostering this collaborative culture is critical to forging strategic partnerships that can expand your capabilities and reach. Encourage your team to collaborate, not just in facing challenges but also in seizing opportunities. Because, as we've seen, when we collaborate we don't just grow faster, we grow better, together.

Key 4: Co-create to accelerate

People buy into what they help create. The quickest way to bring people on board with you is to co-create the future with them. This is as true for your team members as it is for your customers, partners and stakeholders. By co-creating, you're building relationships, trust and mutual respect. You're demonstrating that you value others' contributions and you're open to new ideas and different perspectives.

Co-creation is a powerful tool for accelerating change and achieving shared goals. By inviting others to participate in the creation process, you're not only harnessing their unique skills, knowledge and perspectives, but you're also fostering a sense of shared ownership and commitment. When people feel that they've played a part in shaping a decision, strategy or innovation, they're far more likely to buy into it and work hard to ensure its success.

Co-creation requires strong leadership. As a leader, it's your responsibility to create an environment in which co-creation can thrive. This means encouraging open dialogue, fostering collaboration, and providing the necessary resources and support. It also means being willing to listen, learn and adapt.

Co-creation is not always easy; it can be challenging and time-consuming. It requires patience, flexibility and a willingness to share power and control, but the rewards can be substantial. Co-created solutions are often more innovative, robust and sustainable. They benefit from the collective intelligence, creativity and buy-in of the group.

One of the things I love most about facilitating vision and strategy workshops is the opportunity to co-create with amazing leaders who have bright minds and a passion for making things better. I'll always remember being with a leadership team for a three-day off-site vision and strategy workshop in February 2022. On the third day of the workshop, 24-02-2022, Russia invaded Ukraine. In that moment, we had to accept the new current reality of what would become a devastating war, and that business in Europe was changing. We realised that we would need to pivot, quickly. Standing around a large map projected onto the screen, we started brainstorming ideas. What would be the implications of war? What were the current trends we needed to consider? What would be the direction of travel over the next eight to ten years? Everyone contributed to a new strategic action plan for the region. They innovated, communicated and collaborated, and as a result they co-created. That session unlocked opportunities for millions of Euros in annual savings and opened up new trading routes that previously weren't being considered. That's the power of co-creation, even during a crisis.

I've also experienced co-creation at its best, facilitating workshops with a combined team from a multinational groceries and general merchandise retailer and one of their speciality foods suppliers. They set out on a mission to reduce packaging, and at the same time innovate in the category to add more value to consumers, shoppers and their mutually beneficial category. Brainstorming, flip-charting and presenting their ideas side-by-side, they addressed a shared problem with shared goals and values, and co-created a shared solution for the future of the category.

Teams that co-create effectively:

- **Involve stakeholders** – Involving stakeholders in the creation process can lead to better solutions that are more readily accepted, thus accelerating implementation.

- **Encourage customer participation** – Inviting customers to co-create products or services can speed up innovation and increase market acceptance.

- **Enlist cross-functional teams** – Using cross-functional teams for co-creation can speed up the process by reducing the need for extensive coordination across different departments.

- **Create a shared vision** – A shared vision can unify efforts and accelerate the co-creation process.

- **Establish feedback loops** – Establishing quick feedback loops during the co-creation process continuously refines and improves the output, thus accelerating the time to market.

As you seek to accelerate positive change, consider how you can harness the power of co-creation. Who could you invite into your creative process? How could their input enhance your outcomes? How could their involvement increase their commitment to your shared goals? By co-creating your future, you can accelerate your progress and achieve greater success.

Summary

The key to rapid growth and progress lies in your ability to adapt, learn and iterate. By employing design thinking and innovation theory, you can unlock new opportunities and overcome obstacles more effectively.

Stay committed to continuous improvement and embrace the 0–1–100 framework to transform your ideas into tangible results. The journey towards liberating your greatness is an ongoing process. With the power of acceleration on your side, you will be well prepared to conquer any challenge and reach the heights of success you aspire to achieve. Innovate, communicate, collaborate and co-create to accelerate from 0–1–100 – that's the Principle of Acceleration.

Practical application

Reflect on the Principle of Acceleration

Reflection is a skill. Take a moment to capture your thoughts and commit to taking consistent action to move the needle forward.

- What key insights did you discover in this chapter?

- What decisions are you committed to making to gain the greatest return?

- What disciplined action will you take in the next week/month/quarter that will give you the greatest reward?

Activity

In the spirit of striving for excellence and continual improvement, what will you...

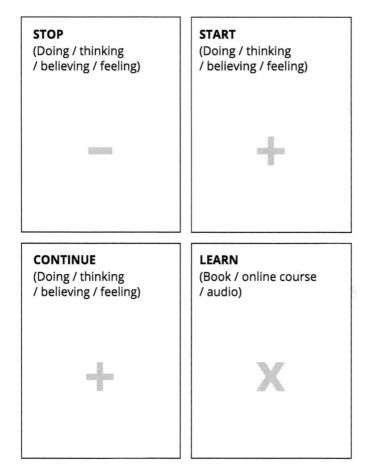

STOP
(Doing / thinking
/ believing / feeling)

START
(Doing / thinking
/ believing / feeling)

CONTINUE
(Doing / thinking
/ believing / feeling)

LEARN
(Book / online course
/ audio)

Additional resources

For bonus videos and downloadable content related to the Principle of Acceleration, visit: www.liberateyourgreatness.com/acceleration.

Conclusion
It's just the beginning:
Live a life of greatness

As we conclude this journey through the pages of *Liberate Your Greatness*, it's time to embrace your potential as a business leader or entrepreneur and take the leap into a life of greatness. The lessons and principles shared in this book have equipped you with the tools and mindset to make a lasting impact in your personal and professional lives. Greatness is a pursuit; it's a journey to becoming extraordinary.

In my head, I want you to thrive personally and professionally. Whether you're a leader in a large corporate organisation, a business owner, an entrepreneur, a team leader or a leader in your community or family, I want you to achieve your goals faster, accelerate your growth and amplify the impact you can have in and through your organisation – and beyond. In my heart, I want you to be the truly authentic best version of yourself, enhancing your relationships and creating quality experiences with those you care about most.

The six core principles of the Liberating Greatness Framework serve as a compass to guide you on this path to success in all areas of your life:

1. **The Principle of Awareness** has taught you that change starts with awareness. Clarity brings peace, purpose and passion. Begin by understanding where you are, identifying your strengths and areas of growth, and recognising the opportunities that lie ahead.

2. **The Principle of Alignment** emphasises the importance of aligning your vision, purpose, mission, values and people to create an unstoppable force driving you towards success. Congruence and consistency are key. Ensure that every aspect of your life and business is in harmony and moving in the same direction.

3. **The Principle of Action** reminds you that your success lies in your activities. Remember that your answer is always in your activity. Step out of your comfort zone and be courageous in taking meaningful steps towards your goals. Trust the process and trust that your efforts will lead to the desired outcome.

4. **The Principle of Accountability** underscores the value of holding yourself and your team accountable for your actions and decisions. Nothing challenges you to level up more than accountability. Embrace a culture of responsibility and ownership, knowing that it will propel you to new heights.

5. **The Principle of Amplification** inspires you to lead people, manage systems and leverage your influence to maximise your impact. Your legacy will be written by your ability to connect, inspire, encourage and uplift others to communicate, collaborate and co-create the future. Embrace the power of leading people, managing systems and using your influence to amplify your impact and scale your success. Amplify before you spin the flywheel for even greater impact.

6. **The Principle of Acceleration** encourages you to test, learn and iterate, adopting an agile approach to growth. Embrace innovation, communication, collaboration and co-creation to go from 0 to 1 to 100, transforming your business and personal lives at an exponential pace.

As a business leader or entrepreneur, you are called to make a difference in the world. You can create lasting change and inspire greatness in others. It's time to step up and live a life that reflects the greatness within you.

Take the lessons you've learnt from the Liberating Greatness Framework and put them into practice. Commit to a lifetime of learning, growing and striving for excellence in all areas of your life, knowing that your journey will be full of challenges, victories and opportunities to make a difference.

Now is the time to act. Believe in yourself and your potential to create a legacy of greatness. Embrace the challenges and uncertainties that come with the pursuit of success and face them with courage, resilience and determination.

As Marianne Williamson said, 'As we let our own light shine, we unconsciously give other people permission to do the same. As we are liberated from our own fear, our presence automatically liberates others.'[90]

When my work on earth is done, I want to hear the words from Matthew 25:23, 'Well done good and faithful servant.'[91] That's one of the most challenging lines that I think about often. I find myself constantly falling short of my own expectations and at the same time grateful for God's love, mercy and grace, and for another day to give it another go.

This is your moment to rise and shine. Together, we can create a world where business leaders, entrepreneurs and their people thrive, innovate and co-create a brighter, more prosperous future for all. The world needs you to liberate your greatness. Your family, friends, team and business need you to liberate your greatness. I need you to liberate your greatness. By doing so, you'll help me fulfil my purpose.

I want to invite you to share your own story of greatness with the me and our community, so that we can celebrate your journey, failing forward to success. Email us on success@fiit4growth.com or support@ johnroussot.com.

In the words of a fellow Greek philosopher, Nikos Kazantzakis, 'You have your brush and colours, you paint paradise, then in you go!'[92] It's time to liberate your greatness, share it with the world and inspire others to do the same.

Next steps: From insight to implementation to impact

Life – and business – is not meant to be done alone. If you're ready to take the next step and accelerate your progress, my team and I would be honoured to walk alongside you as you liberate your greatness. Knowledge is amplified when applied.

Here are two options for you to consider if you want to build on the initial momentum you've created by reading this book.

DIY (Do It Yourself)

Armed with the principles and strategies outlined in this book, you are well equipped to take the first steps on your path to greatness. You may want to start by identifying the areas you wish to improve, setting DREAM Goals, committing to making marginal gains through disciplined daily action and implementing the strategies that resonate with you most.

Don't forget to track your progress. We've created an online community where you can share your journey, engage with others who are on the same path and find additional resources. Visit our website and join the community forum for interactive discussion boards, Q&A sessions and exclusive content: www.liberateyourgreatness.com/community.

Remember that mastery and transformation take time. Be inspired and enjoyed the journey. Continue to study and practice the six principles and you will make steady progress.

DWY (Done With You)

If you want a more hands-on approach and you're ready to get immersed in a growth environment designed to fast track your results, my team and I are ready to serve you. We offer workshops, webinars, training courses and coaching programmes designed to guide you through the process of liberating your greatness. These sessions provide personalised guidance, practical exercises and group discussions that will boost your learning experience. We will help you craft a personal development plan, provide regular check-ins to track your progress, and offer targeted advice to help you overcome your specific challenges. You can register for these programmes through our website. Additionally, our monthly newsletter provides ongoing support and resources. Make sure to subscribe for updates: www. liberateyourgreatness.com/fast-track.

Let's be clear, DFY (Done For You) is not an option. No one can do this for you. You must be actively involved in liberating your greatness. Consider DIY or DWY again (said with a hug and a push).

Regardless of the path you choose, remember this journey is about your growth and potential. Take advantage of these resources and remember that you're not alone. Whether you're taking this on solo, in tandem with us or letting us guide you every step of the way, we're here to support and serve you. Your greatness is within you, waiting to be unleashed, so let's take these next steps together, accelerating your growth, achieving your goals and amplifying your impact.

Your #OnePositiveAction challenge

We live in an era of transformation, where we're constantly urged to keep up with the accelerating pace of change. While this can seem overwhelming, let's remember that within this whirlwind of change lies a wealth of opportunities to learn, grow and make a difference. I believe strongly in the idea: 'If it doesn't challenge you, it won't change you.'[93] My team and I have created a challenge to help you proactively make change happen.

The #OnePositiveAction challenge is simple. Each day, make a conscious effort to introduce one positive change into your life or the life of someone else. This could be anything: a new action, habit, mindset, skill or way of interacting with others. It could be linked to a personal goal to improve your health, wealth or relationships. It could be a professional goal to lead at a higher level, be a better role model or make an even greater impact. It could be something you would like to do in your community or for your family and friends. Make sure that this change is positive – something that will contribute to your personal or professional growth or the well-being of those around you.

Imagine the potential impact if you were to introduce a single positive change every day. In a week you would have made seven changes; in a month, thirty; in a year, over three hundred… and that's just the beginning. The ripple effect of these changes could reach far beyond your immediate circle, influencing the lives of countless others in ways you may never even see.

This challenge may seem daunting, but remember, the journey of a thousand miles begins with a single step. The trick is to start small. Don't underestimate the power of a single positive action, no matter how insignificant it may seem. A kind word, a helping hand, a shared insight – these seemingly trivial actions can have a ripple effect, spreading positivity and fostering a culture of kindness and understanding. Start with small, manageable tasks, celebrate your victories, treat your setbacks as setups and learn by failing forward. Over time, these small changes will accumulate, leading to significant growth and transformation.

In taking up this challenge, you are not just improving your own life; you are becoming a catalyst for positive change in your environment. You are inspiring others to follow suit and make their own changes, creating a cycle of positivity and growth that can spread far and wide. A single pebble can create ripples across an entire pond; a single spark can start a roaring fire; a single positive change can be the catalyst for a life of growth, fulfilment and success.

I believe in you and your ability to lead positive change. Your journey starts today, with a single step, a single change. Take that step today, and every day that follows, and watch as the power of one positive action transforms not only your life but the world around you. Let's start a movement that echoes across the world.

Embrace the challenge. Unlock your potential, overcome your obstacles and achieve your goals. Start today, and let every day be an opportunity to make a difference, to learn something new, to grow.

Use the hashtag #OnePositiveAction and tag me on LinkedIn, Instagram or Facebook. My team and I would love to celebrate the positive impact you're making in your own life and the lives of all those around you.

Your coach and friend,
John

Notes

1 JC Maxwell, *The 21 Irrefutable Laws of Leadership: Follow them and people will follow you* (HarperCollins, 2007)
2 JF Kennedy, 'Remarks in Heber Springs, Arkansas, at the dedication of Grers Ferry Dam' (3 October 1963), online by G Peters and JT Woolley, *The American Presidency Project*, https://presidency.ucsb.edu/node/236260, accessed 23 June 2023
3 L Buscaglia, *Love: What life is all about* (Slack Incorporated, 1972)
4 G Yocom, 'My shot: Gary Player', *Golf Digest* (31 May 2002), www.golfdigest.com/story/myshot_gd0210, accessed 16 June 2023
5 W Shakespeare, 'Twelfth Night', in S Greenblatt (ed), *The Norton Shakespeare* (W. W. Norton & Co, 2008)
6 'The Global Goals', https://globalgoals.org, accessed 23 June 2023
7 *The Bible, New King James Version* (Thomas Nelson Publishers, 1975)
8 A Robbins, *Awaken the Giant Within: Take immediate control of your mental, emotional, physical and financial destiny* (Simon & Schuster, 1992)
9 CS Dweck, *Mindset: The new psychology of success* (Random House, 2007)
10 A Goldberg, *Be Your Truth* (Lulu, 2019)
11 A Middleton, *Mental Fitness: 15 rules to strengthen your body and mind* (HarperCollins, 2021)
12 M Forleo, *Everything Is Figureoutable* (Penguin Publishing Group, 2019)
13 Quotes.net, 'Socrates quotes', https://quotes.net/quote/925, accessed 23 June 2023
14 M Gladwell, *Outliers: The Story of Success* (Little, Brown and Company, 2008)
15 K Anders Ericsson, MJ Prietula and ET Cokely, 'The making of an expert', *Harvard Business Review* (July–August 2007), https://hbr.org/2007/07/the-making-of-an-expert, accessed 16 June 2023

16 B Lee, *Tao of Jeet Kune Do* (Ohara Publications, 1975)

17 B Lee, '#2 Be water, my friend' *Bruce Lee Podcast*, https://brucelee.com/podcast-blog/2016/7/20/2-be-water-my-friend, accessed 16 June 2023

18 TM Amabile and SJ Kramer, *The Progress Principle: Using small wins to ignite joy, engagement, and creativity at work* (Harvard Business Review Press, 2011)

19 M Slater, 'Olympics cycling: Marginal gains underpin team GB dominance' *BBC Sport* (8 August 2012), https://bbc.co.uk/sport/olympics/19174302, accessed 16 June 2023

20 T Hsieh, *Delivering Happiness: A path to profits, passion, and purpose* (Grand Central Publishing, 2010)

21 'Awareness', *Oxford English Dictionary* (Oxford University Press, 2022), retrieved 15 April 2022

22 Z Ziglar, *You Don't Have To Be Great To Start, But You Have To Start To Be Great* (Independently published, 2021)

23 J Luft and H Ingham, 'The Johari Window, A Graphic Model of Interpersonal Awareness', *Proceedings of the Western training laboratory in group development* (UCLA, 1955)

24 E Hamre, 'How Kobe outworked the rest to go from summer league failure to 5× NBA champion' *Medium.com* (9 March 2020), https://medium.com/skilluped/how-kobe-outworked-the-rest-to-go-from-summer-league-failure-to-5x-nba-champion-773602807e71, accessed 22 June 2023

25 'Self-Awareness', *Oxford English Dictionary* (Oxford University Press, 2022), retrieved 18 April 2022

26 'Character', *Oxford English Dictionary* (Oxford University Press, 2022), retrieved 18 April 2022

27 F Deltour, *The Secrets of Socrates: Quotes & philosophy* (Frederic Deltour, 2017)

28 The Myers-Briggs Company, 'The Myers-Briggs Type Indicator® (MBTI®) assessment', https://eu.themyersbriggs.com/en/tools/MBTI, accessed 19 June 2023

29 DiSC Profile, 'What is DiSC®?', https://discprofile.com/what-is-disc, accessed 19 June 2023

30 Gallup CliftonStrengths®, 'Live your best life using your strengths', https://gallup.com/cliftonstrengths, accessed 19 June 2023

31 The Enneagram Institute®, 'The nine enneagram type descriptions', https://enneagraminstitute.com/type-descriptions, accessed 19 June 2023

32 SR Covey, *The 7 Habits of Highly Effective People: Powerful lessons in personal change* (Simon & Schuster, 1989)

33 K Blanchard, P Zigarmi and D Zigarmi, *Leadership and the One Minute Manager: Increasing effectiveness through situational leadership* (HarperCollins, 2013)

34 M Goedert, '"If you want to go fast, go alone, if you want to go far, go together". African Proverb', College of Public Health (8 September 2016), https://blog.unmc.edu/publichealth/2016/09/08/if-you-want-to-go-fast-go-alone-if-you-want-to-go-far-go-together-african-proverb-martha-goedert, accessed 19 June 2023

35 B Noble, personal communication with the author

36 M Johnson, 'Aku', *Aku World* (2022), https://aku.world, accessed 19 June 2023

37 M Johnson, 'A letter from the creator', *Aku World* (2022), www.aku.world/area21/letter-from-micah-johnson, accessed 19 June 2023

38 VE Frankl, *Man's Search for Meaning* (Beacon Press, 1959)

39 *Parable of the Three Bricklayers* (n.d.), retrieved from common knowledge

40 M Winn, https://marcwinn.com, accessed 20 June 2023

41 Based on the ikigai framework, with copyright permission from Marc Winn

42 *The King James Bible*, www.kingjamesbibleonline.org, accessed 20 June 2023

43 Joe Marais' art can be purchased at: https://singulart.com/en/artist/joe-marais-11945

44 N Kazantzakis, *Zorba the Greek* (Simon & Schuster, 1952)

45 S Bartlett, 'Episode 155: Bear Grylls: Man VS Failure, Anxiety & Imposter Syndrome' *The Diary of a CEO with Steven Bartlett* (27 June 2022), https://podcasts.apple.com/gb/podcast/the-diary-of-a-ceo-with-steven-bartlett/id1291423644, accessed 20 June 2023

46 *The Bible, New International Version*, https://biblegateway.com, accessed 20 June 2023

47 Daddy Saturday, www.daddysaturday.com, accessed 20 June 2023

48 I Nitobe, *Bushido: The soul of Japan* (Teibi Publishing Company, 1899)

49 JA Barker, 'The power of vision' (1991), https://youtube.com/watch?v=LVONMxCK4CQ, accessed 20 June 2023

50 GT Doran, 'There's a S.M.A.R.T. way to write management's goals and objectives', *Management Review*, 70/11 (1981), 35–36, https://community.mis.temple.edu/mis0855002fall2015/files/2015/10/S.M.A.R.T-Way-Management-Review.pdf, accessed 20 June 2023

51 N Mandela, 'It always seems impossible until it's done' (2020), https://youtube.com/watch?v=RmBEpRW01pI, accessed 20 June 2023

52 M Minnicks, 'Nothing happens until something moves' *Letterpile* (23 June 2019), https://letterpile.com/religion/Nothing-Happens-Until-Something-Moves, accessed 20 June 2023

53 D Johnson (@TheRock) 'And always be the hardest worker in the room…' (7 August 2014), https://twitter.com/therock/status/497443660355481600?lang=da, accessed 20 June 2023

54   PB Brown, "'You miss 100% of the shots you don't take." You need to start shooting at your goals', *Forbes* (12 January 2014), https://forbes.com/sites/actiontrumpseverything/2014/01/12/you-miss-100-of-the-shots-you-dont-take-so-start-shooting-at-your-goal/?sh=6d293b446a40, accessed 20 June 2023

55   J Rohn (@JimRohnBot) 'Indecision is the thief of opportunity' (16 September 2021), https://twitter.com/JimRohnBot/status/1438374788309950468, accessed 20 June 2023

56   *The Bible, New International Version*, https://biblegateway.com, accessed 20 June 2023

57   A Robbins, *Personal Power II: The driving force* (Anthony Robbins Productions, 1986)

58   S Furtick, 'Make peace with your strength' (2023), https://youtu.be/Qmy0QvcbhpA, 50:58, accessed 20 June 2023

59   DR Katz, *Just Do It: The Nike spirit in the corporate world* (Random House, 1994)

60   G Wickman, *Traction: Get a grip on your business* (BenBella Books, 2007)

61   A Hormozi, *$100M Offers: How to make offers so good people feel stupid saying no* (Acquisition.com Publishing, 2021)

62   D Washington, 'Denzel Washington on "dreams without goals…"' (2022), https://youtube.com/watch?v=CmgEWKylel4, accessed 20 June 2023

63   D Hardy, *The Compound Effect: Jumpstart your income, your life, your success* (Vanguard Press, 2010)

64   GE Smith, 'Newton's Laws of Motion', in E Schliesser and C Smeenk (eds), *The Oxford Handbook of Newton* (Oxford Academic, 2017), https://doi.org/10.1093/oxfordhb/9780199930418.013.35, accessed 20 June 2023

65   Matthew 25:21, *The Bible, New International Version*, https://biblegateway.com, accessed 20 June 2023

66   K Weliever, 'God will see', *The Preachers Word* (1 November 2022), https://thepreachersword.com/2022/11/01/god-will-see, accessed 21 June 2023

67   M Brodinsky, 'Farewell/it's possible: It's just about… life', *HuffPost* (15 December 2015), www.huffpost.com/entry/farewellits-possible-its_b_8707574, accessed 21 July 2023

68   R Scott, *Gladiator* (Universal Pictures and DreamWorks Pictures, 2000)

69   J Collins, *Good to Great: Why some companies make the leap… and others don't* (Harper Business, 2001)

70   A Pentland, 'The new science of building great teams', *Harvard Business Review* 90/4 (April 2012), 60–69

71   S Sinek, D Mead and P Docker, *Find Your Why: A practical guide for discovering purpose for you and your team* (Portfolio Penguin, 2017)

72 ME Gerber, *The E-Myth Revisited: Why most small businesses don't work and what to do about it* (HarperCollins, 1995)

73 G Wickman, *Traction: Get a grip on your business* (BenBella Books, 2007)

74 D and J Benham, *Expert Ownership: Launching faith-filled entrepreneurs into greater freedom and success* (Benham Media, 2020)

75 D Lama, D Tutu and D Abrams, *The Book of Joy: Lasting happiness in a changing world* (Avery, 2016)

76 U Brunforte, *The Little Flowers of St Francis of Assisi* (Start Publishing, 2013)

77 Arla, 'Our vision', https://arla.com/company/strategy/vision, accessed 21 June 2023

78 Pep Unlimited LLC, 'Albert Einstein: "We cannot solve our problems with the same thinking we used when we created them"' (12 September 2022), https://pepunlimited.com/business/albert-einstein-problem-solving, accessed 21 June 2023

79 F Wilczek, 'Einstein's parable of quantum insanity', *Scientific American* (23 September 2015), www.scientificamerican.com/article/einstein-s-parable-of-quantum-insanity, accessed 21 June 2023

80 N Fleming 'VARK: A guide to learning styles' (1987), http://vark-learn.com, accessed 22 June 2023

81 FL Dyer and TC Martin, *Edison: His life and inventions* (Harper & Brothers Publishers, 1910)

82 S Bartlett, 'Episode 161: Coinbase founder: The crazy journey of building a $100 billion company: Brian Armstrong', *The Diary of a CEO with Steven Bartlett* (18 July 2022), https://podcasts.apple.com/gb/podcast/the-diary-of-a-ceo-with-steven-bartlett/id1291423644, accessed 23 June 2023

83 A Kalumut, 'Nike "Failure" Michael Jordan ad 1997' (2019), https://youtube.com/watch?v=nvrbQBI4ElI, accessed 22 June 2023

84 JK Rowling, 'The fringe benefits of failure', TED (5 June 2008), https://ted.com/talks/jk_rowling_the_fringe_benefits_of_failure, accessed 22 June 2023

85 N Gabler, *Walt Disney: The triumph of the American imagination* (Alfred A Knopf, 2006)

86 Deloitte Digital, 'Ten types of innovation', www.deloittedigital.com/us/en/offerings/customer-led-marketing/customer-strategy-and-applied-design/applied-design-and-innovation/ten-types accessed 22 June 2023

87 L Keeley, H Walters, R Pikkel and B Quinn, *Ten Types of Innovation: The discipline of building breakthroughs* (Wiley, 2013)

88 O Winfrey (@Oprah) 'Dr. Maya Angelou once said…' (26 March 2021), https://twitter.com/Oprah/status/1375251989739663363, accessed 22 June 2023

89 BW Tuckman, 'Developmental sequence in small groups', *Psychological Bulletin*, 63/6 (1965), 384–399, https://doi.org/10.1037/h0022100

90 M Williamson, *A Return to Love: Reflections on the principles of a course in miracles* (Harper Thorsons, 1992)

91 *The Bible, New International Version*, https://biblegateway.com, accessed 22 June 2023

92 N Kazantzakis, *Report to Greco* (Bruno Cassirer, 1965)

93 J Dsouza, 'If it doesn't challenge you, it won't change you' *Lifeism* (14 October 2022), https://lifeism.co/if-it-doesnt-challenge-you-it-wont-change-you, accessed 22 June 2023

Further Resources

In the journey towards liberating your greatness, I am committed to being your ally and guide. As such, I believe in sharing the best resources available, irrespective of their origin, to facilitate your growth and development. I understand that everyone's path is unique, and multiple perspectives can enrich that journey, which is why I've curated this collection of further information and resources.

These materials have been instrumental in my own growth and come highly recommended by experts and peers alike. My goal is to empower you with diverse, high-quality tools and insights, so you can continue to evolve, improve and achieve your own definition of greatness.

Mindset/skillset/toolset

Dweck, CS, *Mindset: The new psychology of success* (Random House, 2007)

Forleo, M, *Everything is Figureoutable* (Penguin Publishing Group, 2019)

Middleton, A, *Mental Fitness: 15 rules to strengthen your body and mind* (HarperCollins, 2021)

Suzuki, S, *Zen Mind, Beginner's Mind* (Shambhala, 2011)

Habits

Burchard, B, *High Performance Habits: How extraordinary people become that way* (Hay House, 2017)

Clear, J, *Atomic Habits: Tiny changes, remarkable results* (Random House Business, 2018)

Covey, S, *The 7 Habits of Highly Effective People: Powerful lessons in personal change* (Simon & Schuster, 1989)

Hardy, D, *The Compound Effect: Jumpstart your income, your life, your success* (Vanguard Press, 2010)

Leadership and business strategy

Amabile, TM, and Kramer, SJ, *The Progress Principle: Using small wins to ignite joy, engagement, and creativity at work* (Harvard Business Review Press, 2011)

Collins, J, *Good To Great: Why some companies make the leap… and others don't* (Harper Business, 2001)

Maxwell, JC, *The 21 Irrefutable Laws of Leadership: Follow them and people will follow you* (HarperCollins, 2007)

Awareness

Blanchard, K, *Leadership and the One Minute Manager: Increasing effectiveness through situational leadership* (HarperCollins, 1999)

Johnson, S, *Who Moved My Cheese? An amazing way to deal with change in your work and in your life* (Vermilion, 1999)

Alignment

García, H, and Miralles, F, *Ikigai: The Japanese secret to a long and happy life* (Hutchinson, 2017)

The Bible (King James Version, New International Version and English Standard Version)

Warren, R, *What on Earth Am I Here For? The purpose driven life* (Zondervan, 2013)

Action

Knight, P, *Shoe Dog: A memoir by the creator of Nike* (Simon & Schuster, 2016)

Sinek, S, *Start with Why: How great leaders inspire everyone to take action* (Penguin, 2011)

Wickman, G, *Traction: Get a grip on your business* (BenBella Books, 2012)

Accountability

Kerr, J, *Legacy: What the All Blacks can teach us about the business of life* (Constable, 2013)

Schmidt, E, Rosenberg, J, and Eagle, A, *Trillion Dollar Coach: The leadership handbook of Silicon Valley's Bill Campbell* (John Murray, 2019)

Amplification

Leruste, M, *Glow in the Dark: How sharing your personal story can transform your business and change your life* (John Murray, 2022)

Priestley, D, *Key Person of Influence: The five-step method to become one of the most highly valued and highly paid people in your industry* (Rethink Press, 2014)

Sullivan, D, and Hardy, B, *Who Not How: The formula to achieve bigger goals through accelerating teamwork* (Hay House, 2020)

Acceleration

Knapp, J, Zeratsky, J, and Kowitz, B, *Sprint: How to solve big problems and test new ideas in just five days* (Simon & Schuster, 2016)

Kurzweil, R, *The Singularity Is Near: When humans transcend biology* (Duckworth, 2006)

Thiel, P, and Masters, B, *Zero to One: Notes on startups, or how to build the future* (Virgin Books, 2015)

Acknowledgements

I would like to express my sincere gratitude and appreciation to all those who have contributed to the writing of this book, which has been a three-year project and the result of twenty years' worth of accumulated experiences. I'm grateful for the journey.

In the grand tapestry of life, there are many threads that intertwine, connecting us in ways that shape our journey and define our experiences. The creation of *Liberate Your Greatness* is no exception. This endeavour has not been a solo journey but a collective effort, woven together with support, guidance and inspiration from many remarkable individuals. The content has come from insights and experiences I've gathered from numerous sources, and has formed through relationships, collaborations and shared wisdom from an extraordinary community.

This community starts with my family, my pillars of strength, love and unwavering support. To my parents, I'll always be grateful for your unconditional love and for instilling in me the values of hard work, resilience and determination from a young age. To my wife, Daleen, and our children, Jewel, Anthony and Marcus, thank you for your patience, encouragement and for being the constant reminder of my 'why'. I am so blessed to have you in my life. You inspire me to *be* more, to *do* more, and to *give* more. Your belief in me fuels my desire to create a better world for you and the generations to come. To my siblings, Riki, Stu and family, and Mark, Nerea and family, thank you too for your love, support and encouragement. To my extended family, thank you for always cheering me on.

Next, I'd like to extend my deep gratitude to my mentors, colleagues and friends. Your wisdom and shared experiences have provided invaluable lessons and perspectives, shaped my thinking, and contributed to the essence of this book.

Special thanks to Brendon Burchard, who opened my eyes to possibilities and the urgency for me to step up and serve at a higher level. You've inspired me, trained me and equipped me to succeed at the highest heights. I'll be forever grateful. Thank you too for the opportunities that you, Randy Garn, and your teams at GrowthDay and the High Performance Institute, have provided for me and FiiT4GROWTH to learn, grow and serve together.

To Darren Hardy, thank you for your guidance through the pandemic, and for pointing me in the direction of my call to adventure on the Hero's Journey. I'm on the path, enjoying the experience, doing my best to inspire hope for a better future and being the exception every step of the way.

To Daniel Priestley and the Dent Global team, the KPI programme has been one of the most impactful I have ever experienced. Thank you for equipping me with the insights, strategies and roadmap required for me to become a Key Person of Influence. I'm still a 'work in progress' as I continue to apply everything you've taught me... watch this space!

To Anthony Trucks, Mark Leruste, Sophie Milliken and Julia Langkraehr, thank you for your coaching and guidance. Each of you has had a unique impact on my personal and professional life. I'm grateful that our paths crossed, and I'm excited about the journey we're on together.

To Ant Middleton, thank you for your support, positive challenge and push for me to level up, demonstrate courage and get the job done, signed, sealed and delivered. I appreciate you and look forward to future adventures together.

To all of the forty-plus coaches and mentors I've had over the years. I have learnt something from each of you that I'll carry and share wherever I go.

To all my clients, past and present. As iron sharpens irons, you make me better – every session, every interaction. I'm grateful for the opportunity to serve you and help you achieve your goals. Thank you for inspiring me every day. I appreciate your trust and value our relationship.

I owe a special note of thanks to my writing and publishing team. To my book coaches, Amelia Forczak and your team at Pithy Wordsmithery, thank you for your guidance and structure that helped me start this journey and for your encouragement throughout my writing process. To my editors, Kathy Steeden and Beth Dymond, whose keen eyes and constructive feedback have added polish and precision to my words. To my publisher, whose faith in this project and professional guidance have made this dream a reality. Lucy McCarraher, Joe Gregory and your team at Rethink Press, thank you for equipping me with the framework, structure and process to plan, write and publish my book. I'm grateful to be part of the Rethink Press portfolio.

To my friends and team who offered to beta read my manuscript, thank you for your objective perspective and input. Special thanks to Ross Butler for investing your time to read and apply your editing superpower to tighten up the first draft of my manuscript. Thank you to Bill Noble, Toby Hone, Ellie Bryan, Matt Read, Shaun Lewarne and Arthur Stamatis. The book is better because of you. I appreciate you all.

Lastly, I am grateful to you, the reader. You who seek to learn, grow and liberate your greatness. Your pursuit of personal and professional excellence makes this book meaningful. Thank you for allowing me to be a part of your journey towards greatness.

In each and every one of you, I see a thread of greatness that has contributed to the making of this book. I am profoundly grateful for your support, for without you, *Liberate Your Greatness* would not exist as it does today. Thank you.

The Author

John Roussot is the founder and CEO of FiiT4GROWTH, a renowned business coaching and online training platform that helps individuals and organisations unlock their full potential. With more than twenty-two years of experience in coaching, mentoring and guiding people towards personal and professional success, John has established himself as a multi-award-winning business coach and leadership development trainer.

John's passion for empowering others began early in his career as he quickly realised the power of positive energy and enthusiasm, focused and inspired action, and the benefits of holistic well-being in driving success. Having worked with individuals, teams and businesses in thirty-three countries, John synthesises global best practices into easy-to-understand frameworks, strategies and tools.

A lifelong learner, John is passionate about his personal development, loves reading and learning through online programmes and proactively seeks input from his coaches and mentors to constantly learn and grow. He is an engaging international speaker, regularly delivering workshops, seminars and keynotes on topics such as liberating greatness, high performance, raising future leaders, the work-life balance graphic equaliser, setting DREAM Goals and making common sense common practice.

When he's not helping others achieve their goals, John enjoys spending time with his family, exploring the great outdoors and staying active through running, gym training and Spartan obstacle course racing. His personal purpose is liberating greatness for individuals, teams and businesses, and he's on a mission to help one million people take #OnePositiveAction.

Connect with John Roussot on LinkedIn, follow him on Twitter and visit his websites to learn more about his coaching services and online training programmes.

🌐 www.fiit4growth.com | www.johnroussot.com | www.liberateyourgreatness.com

🔗 https://uk.linkedin.com/in/johnroussot

📘 https://facebook.com/john.roussot

🐦 @JohnRoussot

ⓖ @johnroussot

📷 @johnroussot